Paul's appeal in 2 Corinthians that believers keep persevering with the ministry of gospel proclamation, even though it is dismissed as weak, is hugely relevant today. In an age in which substance often gives way to style, we urgently need teaching like this, which builds convictions about the nature and power of authentic gospel ministry and spurs us to stick with it.

VAUGHAN ROBERTS,
Rector of St Ebbe's, Oxford and Director of The Proclamation Trust

Imagine a dynamic church ministry built on down to earth teaching. Or what about extraordinary gospel work through very ordinary people. That's what the authors have tried to model in their own lives. And more importantly, it's precisely the plan God lays out for us in 2 Corinthians. These expositions, because they track so clo___ ___ f Scripture, are full of sane, sou ___ highly, both as examples of f reminder that all lasting mini

Senior Pastor, University

This is a breath of fresh air. Most ___ ___ because I have begun to imagine that it depends on my performance. This book has driven me back to the fundamentals and reminded me where the true power lies. It is easy to read, clear and desperately relevant in our culture.

JONTY ALLCOCK,
Lead Pastor, The Globe Church, London

Few New Testament books are more relevant to our contemporary society, which is obsessed by celebrity, status and success, than 2 Corinthians. Whilst many church leaders are capitulating to this culture, William Taylor and David Dargue passionately urge us to have confidence in the "weak" ministry of gospel proclamation. Combining characteristically clear exegesis, relevant application and personal testimony, they explain that an authentic gospel ministry must be cross-shaped and Spirit dependent. This timely book is both a vital warning and a positive ministry manifesto. It will challenge and encourage gospel ministers to press on with the task of preaching Christ, embrace weakness and guard against the temptation to compromise message or method to achieve greater success, respectability, popularity or comfort. It will help church members to appreciate authentic ministry and resist the seductive attractions of false teachers who have accommodated the gospel to the expectations of the culture, thereby undermining its glory and saving power."

JOHN STEVENS,
National Director, Fellowship of Independent Evangelical Churches,
Market Harborough, Leicestershire

In a time of rising hostility towards Christianity in the West, and confusion within many churches as to their central purpose, *Style or Substance? The Nature of True Christian Ministry* provides glorious, bracing, God-given truth to shape and sustain Christian ministry.

Focussing on the central section of Paul's Second Letter to the Corinthians, the book expounds the paradox that is essential to authentic Christian ministry. As the gospel is a message of life through the death of a Crucified Saviour, so the pattern of 'effective' ministry is persevering in the 'weakness' of preaching that gospel - amidst hardship, opposition and humiliation.

This is a book for congregational leaders and prospective congregational leaders certainly, but also for every person who serves in all kinds of word ministry whether in leading groups, teaching children or young people, reading Scripture with inquirers or new believers, or equipping others to serve. The "Questions" at the end of each chapter allow for deep reflection on the truths unfolded and pertinent application of God's truth to our lives and ministries. This is a one volume training course that will deepen joy in the gospel of God and strengthen 'Clay Pot servants' to be at once 'a fragrance from death to death' and 'a fragrance from life to life' (2 Cor. 2:16).

KANISHKA RAFFEL,
Dean of Sydney, Sydney

WILLIAM TAYLOR
& DAVID DARGUE

# STYLE
## OR
# SUBSTANCE?

THE NATURE OF TRUE CHRISTIAN MINISTRY

CHRISTIAN
**FOCUS**
*Good Books with the
Real Message of Hope*

Scripture quotations (marked 'ESV') are taken from the *Holy Bible, English Standard Version*, published by HarperCollins*Publishers* © 2001 Crossway Bibles, a publishing ministry of Good News Publishers. Used by permission. All rights reserved.

Copyright © William Taylor & David Dargue 2016

paperback ISBN 978-1-78191-229-4
epub ISBN 978-1-78191-887-6
mobi ISBN 978-1-78191-888-3

Published in 2016
by
Christian Focus Publications Ltd,
Geanies House, Fearn, Ross-shire,
IV20 1TW, Great Britain.

www.christianfocus.com

Cover design by Pete Barnsley

Printed and bound by
Bell & Bain, Glasgow

MIX
Paper from
responsible sources
FSC® C007785

# Contents

# Preface

IT is our deep conviction that God works in His mighty power by His Spirit through His Word. Jesus puts it that way in John chapter 6 verse 63: *It is the Spirit who gives life; the flesh is no help at all. The words that I have spoken to you are spirit and life.* It is by Jesus' life-giving and eternal Word that His people are born again by the Spirit (1 Pet. 1:23); it is by Jesus' life-giving Word that His people grow up to maturity in salvation (1 Pet. 2:2). When Philip asks to be shown the Father (John 14:8), Jesus' answer is framed in terms of the work of the Spirit in giving us His Word through the Apostles' teaching. Any mighty work of the Spirit of God and any expression of genuine Christian discipleship will have at its very centre the living Word of God. The Bible is the essential bread-and-butter of every Christian's life and growth. Scripture is the vital diet of every healthy church and of every authentic movement of the Spirit. Our desire in writing this book is to help bring the Word of God to the people of God through the simple exposition of that Word.

The book is based on a set of edited talks that were first preached by William on Sunday mornings at St Helen's and then on a number of weekends away in subsequent years. The authorship of this book is built on that dynamic. Unless stated, 'I' is specifically William. It is an immense privilege to serve within church families that are hungry to be taught God's Word, and many of the reflections and discoveries within this book come as a result of conversations and observations made by such members as we have explored the letter together. As with any Bible teaching enterprise, it is very much a 'work in progress'.

We are enormously grateful to Rachel Meek for her thoughtful, careful and gracious work in editing this manuscript. We have been significantly helped both in thinking about the overall flow of the book, and in the details of punctuation and consistency. It transpires that despite numerous opportunities to be schooled in these arts, there still remains room for improvement!

# Introduction

## The Question to Answer

WHENEVER we read a book of the Bible, we are trying to work out the author's purpose in writing. Since the Bible writers were inspired by God, we are then trying to work out God's particular aim in writing. Sometimes Bible writers explicitly tell us why they are writing. At other times we have more detective work to do, hunting through the book for clues. We will want to ask: 'Who is writing? To whom are they writing? What is their situation? Are there particular issues in view? Is there one idea that keeps everything together? Are there repeated themes?'

Having done that work, we will then want to ask the question 'why?'. Why is the Bible author beginning to talk about this particular issue, at this particular point? I take it that this is amongst the most important questions that any Bible teacher asks at any stage in their preparation. 'Why? Why? Why? Why?' The key to preaching and teaching that carries weight is to allow the theology of the author, as he has lined up his theology towards a particular pastoral purpose, to drive the pastoral purpose that you are seeking to achieve. Insofar as I have understood both the theology of the author and its pastoral purpose, which are aligned, then I take it that my preaching and teaching will carry the weight that the Holy Spirit intended it to. But insofar as I misunderstand the theology of the author and then seek to achieve the pastoral purpose, or I misunderstand the pastoral purpose but teach the theology, so far will my preaching be equally less weighty. The Holy Spirit has inspired the authors of the Bible, who are themselves theologians, to put together their theology to achieve a particular pastoral purpose. My job as the Bible teacher is to work out not only 'what is it that the author is teaching?', but also 'what is the pastoral purpose to which it is directed?'

## Themes in 2 Corinthians

As we turn to 2 Corinthians, we find three big word-group themes: *commending*, *boasting*, and *comforting*.

*Comforting* comes primarily in chapters 1 and 7, and shows us that 'weak' ministry brings encouragement, salvation, and thus true 'comfort'.

The *boasting* theme shows us that there is a right boasting: in the Lord, in any influence He has given to us (chapters 7 to 10), and in the weaknesses that He has given to us (chapters 11 to 12); and wrong boasting: as a fool, according to the flesh (chapters 11 and 12).

The *commending* theme presents what initially seem to be contradictory ideas. In places Paul seems to deny the need for human commendation of Christian ministry, whether from himself or others (3:1; 10:12,18; 12:19). However, in other places Paul is openly commending himself to the Corinthians (4:2 and 6:4), and seeking their commendation (12:11).

These themes of commending and boasting unify the letter, and are brought together in chapter 5 verse 12, which I take to be the key verse explaining the purpose of the letter:

> *We are not commending ourselves to you again but giving you cause to boast about us, so that you may be able to answer those who boast about outward appearance and not about what is in the heart.*

There is a kind of ministry to boast in, because there is a kind of ministry that brings true comfort. This kind of ministry appears to be weak, but is the kind of ministry that Paul has embodied, and that he wants to commend to them.

## The Situation in Corinth

*Outward appearance* means literally 'on the face', and it seems that some had got the Christian faith and Christian ministry wrong. They were thinking that it is about what I do and about things on the surface; whereas Paul is saying that it is really about what God does, in the heart. At the start of chapter 11 we get a very brief pen-portrait of those in the church who were getting it wrong:

*I wish you would bear with me in a little foolishness. Do bear with me! For I feel a divine jealousy for you, since I betrothed you to one husband, to present you as a pure virgin to Christ. But I am afraid that as the serpent deceived Eve by his cunning, your thoughts will be led astray from a sincere and pure devotion to Christ.*

*Led astray* here carries the sense of seduction, and Paul is concerned that this young church is going to be seduced away from her true husband by false teachers. They are like a new bride who has already taken significant steps towards starting an affair. Paul betrothed the Corinthian Christians to Christ, he arranged the wedding, but he now fears that they are being led astray.

Chapter 11 verse 4 is instructive about these false teachers:

*For if someone comes and proclaims another Jesus than the one we proclaimed, or if you receive a different spirit from the one you received, or if you accept a different gospel from the one you accepted, you put up with it readily enough.*

Interestingly these false teachers taught Jesus, they taught the Spirit, and they taught the gospel. But, it was a different Jesus, a different Spirit and a different gospel. They are described in chapter 2 verse 17 as *peddlers of God's word*. They had infiltrated the Corinthian church: a church of new Christians who in 1 Corinthians were growing weary of the message of the cross, because it appeared too weak and foolish. This is helpful instruction on false teachers. They do not come with a big neon warning sign saying 'false teacher'. Their deception is more subtle, since they actually speak of Jesus.

This letter is a continuation of a long, significant and complex relationship that Paul has had with the church. Acts 18 recounts Paul's planting of the church in Corinth. 1 Corinthians includes details of two letters that were subsequently exchanged: one written by Paul (1 Cor. 5:9) and their response (1 Cor. 7:1). 1 Corinthians itself was written while there were divisions in the church. Chapter 16 verse 5 reveals Paul's intention to visit after passing through Macedonia, but 2 Corinthians chapter 1 verses 15 to 17 reveal that those plans then changed. Instead a *painful visit* was made (2:1) and a 'severe letter' written (2:4), before good news of the Corinthians came back to Paul through Titus (7:7). However Paul is still nervous that the repentance and obedience which he demanded may not have fully taken place (12:20-21). Thus he writes to draw the Corinthians back to him and his ministry, however painful that might be for them.

## The Purpose of 2 Corinthians

The message of this letter can be summarised as 'be confident in the "weak" ministry of Gospel proclamation.' Paul considers the Corinthians to be distancing themselves from him, and thus from apostolic ministry and the biblical Gospel. The letter appeals for loyalty both to the substance and to the form of authentic ministry. The Corinthians were in danger of shifting, not only from the message of the cross (1 Cor. 1:25), but also from confidence in preaching the message, and from a readiness to embrace a cross-shaped pattern of ministry.

It is as if Paul holds up a plumb-line to our view of authentic Christian ministry, and asks us the question, 'are we building straight?' He sees his ministry as a kind of bench-mark or spirit-level, against which we can conduct a spiritual check-up on our own understanding of Christian service and Christian work. This speaks to those ministering to us, to us as we make choices about which ministries we serve in, and also to our own ministry. Paul does not just want us to look at him and say, 'Fantastic, I'm really glad that Paul's Gospel ministry was authentic,' or even just to say these things of others' ministry today. He wants every Christian to embrace the 'weak' method of Gospel proclamation (5:12), to be unashamed of partnering with 'weak' Christians, and to boast in 'weak' ministers. Paul's expectation is that every individual, church and Christian organisation be proactively, imaginatively and energetically committed to the advance of the Gospel, through the proclamation of the Gospel, for the honour and glory of Jesus. Paul speaks about himself to strengthen the whole church in Corinth (12:19, 13:10), so that the church will be full of people who understand genuine Christian ministry, and in order that they can reach other people themselves. It is in this 'weakness' that God's power is exhibited (12:10). Nothing could be more apposite for our 'celebrity' culture.

## Our Chosen Section

There are five main sections of the letter shown below, with this volume concentrating on the second and main section, chapter 2 verse 14 to chapter 7 verse 4:

1:1–2:13     The comfort of authentic ministry – 'weak' ministry brings salvation

Our chosen section forms a distinct segment within the flow of the letter. On either side of it, Titus and the mention of Paul's journey into Macedonia are in focus (cf. 2:12-13 and 7:5-6). Whilst contributing its own themes, the section is evidently woven into and integral to the rest of the letter, as has been shown by the confluence of word-group themes at chapter 5 verse 12. We are not alone in marking this out as a section, or in seeing the value of expounding it. Barnett suggests that this section is 'arguably, the centrepiece of the entire letter.'[1] Guthrie writes, 'The section reaching from 2:14-7:4 exudes a theological richness and depth of reflection on the nature of Christian ministry unparalleled in the NT.'[2]

There are three broad divisions within the section. Firstly, chapter 2 verse 14 to chapter 4 verse 6 shows the paradigm of ministry. As a triumphal procession, it is simultaneously victorious and humiliating, and brings life to some and death to others. This life comes because of the substance of the ministry: Transformation, Regeneration, Justification, and Illumination, as Paul sets out in chapter 3. Therefore chapter 4 verses 1 to 6 conclude that in light of the significance of this ministry, Paul refuses either to lose heart in the face of setbacks, or to change the message that he has been given. Secondly, chapter 4 verse 7

1. Paul Barnett, *2 Corinthians*, NICOT, 1997, p. 137.

2. George H. Guthrie, *2 Corinthians*, Baker Academic, 2015, p. 150.

to chapter 5 verse 10 explores the themes of suffering and weakness in light of eternity. The hardships that Paul experiences now are not a reason to lose heart. This is because through his sufferings, he is following the pattern of Jesus, life is coming to others, and along with all Christians, he is looking forward to being with the Lord. Thirdly, in chapter 5 verse 11 to chapter 7 verse 4, Paul calls for allegiance both to himself and to the Gospel message and ministry he preaches and practises. He has been entrusted by God with the ministry of reconciliation. Therefore, to be reconciled to God, we must also be reconciled to Paul.

We must be careful that our use of the words 'ministry' and 'minister' accord with that of Paul and the other New Testament writers. The original Greek terms mean simply 'service', and 'servant' or 'one who waits at tables'. Today 'minister' carries overtones of 'position' or 'office', both in Government and in the Church. However, the New Testament meaning is significantly less grand. In Acts 6 verse 2 the infinitive is rendered *to serve tables* (i.e. to be a waiter). In 2 Corinthians chapter 4 verse 5, Paul describes himself as a 'slave' (translated 'servant' in the ESV), having said that he has *this ministry by the mercy of God* (4:1). Both of these examples demonstrate that 'ministry' and being a 'minister' were not exalted activities or positions.

Therefore, throughout this work, 'ministry' and 'service', and 'minister' and 'servant' are used interchangeably. By 'Christian service', we mean Word-centred Bible teaching, encompassing a great range of possibilities. Leading a one-to-one or a small group study, serving on a Christian summer camp, running a crèche so that others can hear the Word proclaimed, giving a talk or being involved in a prison ministry are all included within such Christian service.

## Why This Book?

2 Corinthians was one of the first books that I taught after being appointed as Rector of St Helen's. Among the many benefits teaching

it provided, was the pattern of ministry that it set out before us all to follow. The letter is something to which we return at least every five years at our Leaders' Weekends. The majority of our small-group leaders are men and women in their twenties and thirties, who are getting their first taste of Christian ministry. At such a weekend, they will be in the midst of the inevitable weakness, frustrations and hard labour that such work involves. It is crucial that these leaders are properly taught about what Gospel ministry really is, and what it looks and feels like. More than that, it is vital that in the decades to come, they are able to keep their confidence in the ministry of proclamation that looks weak, but which changes the heart. Many of them will be serving on PCCs or Elderships, and some will be paid Gospel ministers.

The contrast in Corinth was between authentic ministry that changes the heart, and false ministry that was only 'on the face'. Such a contrast exists in church life, because the contemporary culture that is so concerned with the 'on the face' invades the church. The pattern was there in Corinth, and in every age it will be present in some form. There is nothing new under the sun. It has been around for the last thirty years, and will continue to be so. It is therefore of paramount importance that the next generation are clear on the principles set out here, so that they can apply them to future scenarios. This volume is predominantly written to an audience similar to those who have attended the Leaders' weekends: namely, those who have started with the type of ministry set forth in this letter. It is a call to stick with and boast in such a ministry today.

Five contemporary areas can be identified against which this 'defence' is crucial:

**'Spiritual' ministries** appear every few years, claiming to be the next great work of the Holy Spirit. Dramatic events are presented as evidence of the Spirit's work. However, these so-called 'proofs' of a great work of God bear little resemblance to the marks that Paul sets before us in 2 Corinthians.

'**Prosperity' ministries** are currently booming, promising 'your best life now'. The error is often an over-realised eschatology, taking promises made to Christians concerning the time *after* Jesus returns, and pledging them to the believer now. These chapters contain a devastating rebuttal to the idea that the Christian life today should be one of continually improving circumstances.

'**Changed message' ministries** are always around us, and often develop out of a concern to reach more people for Christ. Of course the Gospel should be presented in a culturally appropriate way; but these chapters show us the red lines that cannot be crossed in terms of the content of the message. They also set an expectation of unavoidable opposition and division that result from the proclamation of the message, which some try to avoid at all costs.

'**Try harder' ministries** recognise the need to be changed more and more into the likeness of Christ. However, they suggest the pursuit of this by human effort, frequently with a confidence in patterns and practices of the Old Covenant to achieve the change. 2 Corinthians reminds us that it is the work of the Spirit, together with God's Word, that brings real change.

'**Proclamation less-central' ministries** do not deny or contradict key truths that 2 Corinthians expounds. They would certainly have the proclamation of the Word as part of their meeting. However, they might show greater confidence in things other than God's Word to bring new life and real change. This might be an atmosphere, or style, or humour, or good relationships, or the right venue. Perhaps a social project might be where the greatest excitement and expectation lie, or a leader with his gifts or style of leadership.

# 1

# The Pattern of Authentic Christian Ministry

## 2 Corinthians 2:14-17

*¹⁴ But thanks be to God, who in Christ always leads us in triumphal procession, and through us spreads the fragrance of the knowledge of him everywhere. ¹⁵ For we are the aroma of Christ to God among those who are being saved and among those who are perishing, ¹⁶ to one a fragrance from death to death, to the other a fragrance from life to life. Who is sufficient for these things? ¹⁷ For we are not, like so many, peddlers of God's word, but as men of sincerity, as commissioned by God, in the sight of God we speak in Christ.*

AT the start of this main section of 2 Corinthians, three very simple pictures of genuine, Christ-like ministry are introduced: slavery, sacrifice and sincerity.

## 1. The Slave (v. 14)

The picture of the slave speaks of the extreme cost of genuine Christian ministry, and of the suffering that is experienced by genuine Christian servants, as they engage in proclaiming the message of Jesus.

The language Paul uses is of a triumphal procession. It was the sort of parade seen on Victory in Europe day at the end of the Second

World War in 1945. On occasions like the recent 70th anniversary, pictures are shown of this time when the British forces returned and marched through the streets of London. The scenes were unlike anything our generation has ever really experienced: people cheering, garlands of flowers, rejoicing, women and children climbing up on to tanks and armoured carriers. Champagne, relief, delight and thanksgiving were all around. A little more recently, there were memorable scenes at the end of the Falklands campaign in 1982, as the ships rounded the headland at Portsmouth, with the returning men standing on the decks. The sporting victory parades of today are in a similar vein, whether the FA Cup paraded through a city centre, or Olympic medals being exhibited along The Mall.

Such military parades were commonplace in the ancient world. The book of Jeremiah tells of the sacking of Jerusalem, and how King Nebuchadnezzar dragged both people and plunder back to Babylon. Josephus, the Jewish historian writing in the First Century about the return of the conquering Roman General Vespasian, gives a detailed account of his victory parade. But rather than being a military parade, Paul is speaking of God's parade. God is at the head of it: *Thanks be to **God** who in Christ always leads us in triumphal procession* (our emphasis).

The picture speaks of a parade designed to proclaim to everyone the great and mighty victory of Jesus over sin, death, the world and the devil. The message of the procession is that Jesus, God's Son, has been established in Heaven, as final Lord and Ruler for all time. However, this is not just a picture for Paul's time. As Christians take part in proclaiming this same message today, their ministry should be understood in the same terms. There is therefore an aspect to Christian ministry that is triumphal.

But God's victory has not been achieved without a cost. Like the Victory in Europe parade, behind this ceremony lies a sacrifice: the death of Jesus, a divine sacrifice, enabling believers to enjoy all the benefits of His New Creation.

The victory that God is proclaiming in triumph has at its heart the suffering and death of God's Son. The victory over sin and death and Satan has been won through Jesus' sin-bearing death. His life was one of self-sacrifice, given over to bringing the message of eternal life to humankind. His death was sin-bearing, as He alone satisfied God's wrath at our rebellion and paid the price for our sin. As Jesus' servants join in that procession, and proclaim His death, so they too find themselves sharing in the sacrifice, suffering and hostility that He attracted. Such participation is a mark of genuine ministry. The language of triumphal procession is so apt, because the ritual slaughter of enemy soldiers was a key part of such events. When Nebuchadnezzar sacked Jerusalem in 587 B.C., he led out the captured soldiers as slaves to be slaughtered. When the Emperor Vespasian sacked Jerusalem in 69 A.D., he carried back to Rome vast wealth and riches from the city. There was not a Geneva Convention, nor a Bill of Human Rights, nor war-crimes' investigations to protect the vanquished. At the very end of the procession, as the enemy forces were led through the streets, was the enemy general. As the procession reached the triumphal arch, more often than not, he was slaughtered.

From the context of this letter, it seems that Paul sees himself as part of a triumphal procession, as he did in 1 Corinthians chapter 4 verse 9: *For I think that God has exhibited us apostles as last of all, like men sentenced to death, because we have become a spectacle to the world, to angels, and to men.* He is part of a procession both to death and to resurrection, as he proclaims the death of Christ. In verse 14 Paul sees himself as being triumphantly led in this procession. In verse 15 Paul speaks of the aroma of a sacrificial thank-offering, with his life being given up as the sacrifice. He simultaneously sees himself as a member of the procession proclaiming God's victory, and as a slave in the procession being led to his death. The picture of triumphal procession is therefore deliberately ambiguous.

Dr Paul Barnett, in his commentary on this letter, writes:

'The metaphor is at the same time triumphal and anti-triumphal. It is as God leads His servants *as prisoners of war* in a victory parade that God spreads the knowledge of Christ everywhere through them …. To be sure Paul's ministry is marked by suffering, but so far from disqualifying Paul as a minister, God's leading him *in Christ* as a suffering servant thereby legitimates his ministry. Christ's humiliation in crucifixion is reproduced in the life of His servant.'[1]

This picture then is one of the extreme cost of genuine Christian ministry. Since Christians join in this triumphal procession with and in Christ, so, if they are involved in a ministry that is genuinely proclaiming Christ, they will be engaged in service that is both costly and triumphal.

The recognition of this first aspect of genuine Christian ministry is crucial. One of the main reasons that Christians choose to move away from such a ministry is the extreme cost. As Paul holds up the plumb-line, he tells us that if believers are going to be engaged in genuine Christian ministry, they are going to be slaves! It is tough, it is a procession to death, it is the ministry of a slave and it involves personal sacrifice. If Jesus and the cross are in mind, then the significant troubles experienced in service of Jesus will not come as any surprise.

A survey of the whole letter shows that there are three types of cost that Paul has in mind:

## Hatred and Hostility

As the truth about Jesus Christ is proclaimed – that His death is the only way for people to share in God's future; that He alone is seated at

---

1. Barnett, p. 150.

God's right hand as Lord and Ruler of the world; that He is our final judge – hostility and hatred will be faced, especially from some who claim to be doing genuine ministry. Chapter 10 verse 10 shows us that Paul has experienced this. Experience today proves the principle. This is a pattern for all Christians to be clear on, not just church leaders.

A church and her ministers known well to the authors have over time been given the following names: mullahs of the Church of England; bigots; idealists; fundamentalists; sexist, racist and rich; the Abu Hamza of the Church of England. It should be no surprise. Today, some churches from an evangelical background aspire to be welcomed and loved by the city that surrounds them. This principle of hatred and hostility should temper such expectations.

## Hardship and Hassle

Hardship and hassle highlight the sheer inconvenience of genuine Christian ministry. It may be a matter of time being squeezed. Seemingly better invitations might have to be turned down; there might be less time for favourite hobbies; the social diary might need to be arranged around the particular responsibilities that have been given. There will be all sorts of little decisions to make: perhaps choosing to leave weekend visits to family and friends early in order to prioritise serving at church. For small-group leaders it may be the decision to find the necessary hours of preparation for each study, which is all the more difficult when surrounded by a culture that lives for the 'now'. It may be a decision to be downwardly mobile in order to stay engaged in a particular ministry. It may be a decision to give up on some luxury in order to give time or money to the proclamation of Jesus Christ. It may simply be the extra time and emotional energy involved in sharing Jesus Christ with people who are resistant. Decisions of self-sacrifice, as a result of a desire for selfless service.

Throughout the first two chapters of this letter, Paul is organising and reorganising his diary and appointments, his plans and his decisions, in order to engage in the proclamation of Jesus Christ as Lord. At the end of the letter, he speaks of the hardship and hassle of a *thorn in the flesh* (12:7).

## Heartache and Hard Work

Genuine Christian service will also involve heartache and hard work, which is seen in chapter 11 verse 28. Paul carried the progress of the Corinthian church in his heart, so that if they stumbled, he felt it. If they suffered, he suffered with them. If they were set back, so was he. It might be the distress of seeing couples with whom you have spent significant time when they were younger Christians, now separated. Or it might be the disappointment of seeing someone with whom you have spent years reading the Bible, now having no interest in Christian things at all. There is huge frustration and grief in seeing and experiencing the effects of sin worked out in the lives of those we are serving.

Genuine Christian ministry will look like the ministry of Jesus. False views of such ministry, that deny the great costs, must be avoided. Yet, as Christians are engaged in proclaiming the death of Jesus, it is a glorious triumphal procession! *Thanks be to God who always leads us in triumphal procession.*

## 2. The Sacrifice (vv. 15 to 16)

If the image of slavery speaks of the cost, then the image of sacrifice speaks of the eternal consequence of genuine Christ-like ministry. The language of *aroma* in verse 15 and *fragrance* in verse 16 suggests that Paul has Old Testament burnt offerings in mind. In Genesis 8:21, in relation to Noah's offering, *the LORD smelt the pleasing aroma.* Burnt offerings are described in Exodus 29:18 and Leviticus 1:9 as giving before the LORD *a pleasing aroma*. Paul pictures his service of Jesus in the same way. As he proclaims Christ and gives himself in Christ-like service to others, it is as if his embodiment of the message gives an aroma that operates both vertically and horizontally. Look closely at verse 15:

> *For we are the aroma of Christ* **to God** *among those who are being saved and* **among those** *who are perishing.* (Our emphasis).

## Vertically

As Paul devotes his whole life to God in an offering of grateful and sacrificial worship, so the 'aroma' of his sacrificial service rises vertically to God. God as it were smells it, and immediately recognises the authentic article as an offering to Him. The Genesis, Exodus and Leviticus references show us this vertical dimension. This is a brilliant metaphor, because everyone is used to identifying things immediately by smell. It is a powerfully evocative sense, and whether it is food, or farms, or fragrances, certain smells are inescapable and trigger powerful associations. Here, it is the aroma of Christ that is being 'smelt'.

Paul's ministry is costly, but he does not engage in it reluctantly, or with his heels dragging. All the way through the verses, Paul is full of gratitude and praise. There is no sense of hesitation in his sacrificial service, or of the wretched sin of self-pity, despite the extreme cost. Chapter 1 verse 3, chapter 2 verse 17, chapter 8 verses 2 and 16 all show that to be the case.

Such gratitude and thankfulness in ministry may not always be our experience. It may then be necessary to take some time out, in order to rekindle this sense of thankfulness in our hearts. That might come through dwelling on verses like chapter 5 verse 21, chapter 8 verse 9 or chapter 13 verse 4. Or that might come through writing out 100 things that you are thankful to God for, an exercise that our ministry teams regularly benefit from.

## Horizontally

Horizontally, however, as Paul proclaims the death of Jesus, the message divides those who listen. Genuine Christian ministry that is full of gratitude to God cannot be engaged in without it being divisive. It can be hugely disconcerting, but genuine ministry that is modelled on Jesus always divides.

The Marmite commercials brilliantly recognise and play on the fact that some people detest Marmite, and others are addicted to it. 'You either love it or hate it.' As Paul conducts this genuine ministry of proclaiming the victory of Jesus, the very message of Jesus' death on the cross divides people. This is unlike the expectation of the false teachers who proclaim a false Jesus, a false gospel, and a false Spirit. They seek to come with recommendations from everybody, but Paul is quite clear that the message he proclaims will bring division. Some will be convicted of sin, and will turn to Jesus. Others will take offence at the genuine Gospel message, and will turn away from Jesus.

This is something that all Christians need to understand clearly, to guard against the risk of simply giving up. Many people, who used to be eager servants of Jesus when they were younger, are now silent servants, no longer engaged in genuine service of Christ, because they find the divisiveness too much. But Christian ministry will always operate in two ways: some will be brought to life, others to judgment. This pattern will occur at all levels: from one-to-one Bible studies, to evangelistic courses, among Bible-study groups, and across a whole church. This clear understanding of what happens in ministry enables Paul to keep going when faced with hostile opposition, for not everyone turns away: *to the other a fragrance from life to life* (v. 16).

As he proclaims the crucified Christ and His victory over death, Paul knows that some are raised to eternal life.

## 3. Sincerity (v. 17)

Sincerity pictures the authentic product of genuine Christian ministry. Once again Paul uses an image that everyone can relate to. Dodgy salesmen are commonplace, whether a car dealer trying to charge a premium for a rust-bucket, or a market stall-holder selling counterfeit goods.

Paul says that genuine Christian ministry presents us with a choice about the kind of service we will engage in. The ministry of the peddler offers fake goods that are attractive, but that do not work. It is 'on the face', impressive and draws a crowd. But when the bonnet is lifted, there is nothing there. It is a false gospel, a phony Spirit, and an alternative Jesus. The genuine Gospel worker presents the true Gospel, which impacts the heart and brings about the authentic product of changed lives, to the glory of God.

The language of verse 17 is very powerful. Consider this literal translation: *but as from sincerity, but as from God, in the sight of God, in Christ, we speak*. Paul speaks the message given to him by God, in the sight of God, faithful to God, enabled and indwelt by Jesus, not altering the message. Therefore the product that is formed by his work, as a slave engaged in presenting this sacrifice, is genuine and authentic.

This is an important idea to grasp. Later on in 2 Corinthians, the false teachers are described as being most concerned about their performance in front of their peers, and their own reputation. Paul writes, *they measure themselves by one another and compare themselves with one another* (10:12). In contrast, Paul is only concerned for the opinion of God. He has the message of the Gospel. He serves with his eye on 'the audience of One'. He is not a people-pleaser. He will proclaim only that message that God has given to him. He says in verse 16, *who is sufficient*? The answer is 'we are', because the message from God is powerful to effect change in the hearts of his hearers. Therefore Paul (in 3:3) is able to point to the real change in the lives of the Corinthians, in order to demonstrate that his ministry is authentic.

As Paul speaks of the work of Christ, so the Spirit of the living God inscribes truth on the hearts of those who hear his message. As the Spirit does His work of convincing and convicting, so lives are changed. Those amongst whom Paul ministers become themselves a living, walking, talking advertisement for the authentic ministry that he is engaged in.

## Conclusion

This opening section then presents every leader within a church and every church member with a choice. Authentic Christian ministry will be conducted by men and women who see themselves as 'slaves' in a triumphal procession. The procession's ultimate outcome is triumph – Christ is risen, life is guaranteed! But the procession's immediate experience will be one of sacrifice. There will be hostility and hatred; hardship and hassle; heartache and hard work. This has to be so, for the proclamation of Jesus Christ as Lord, of His death and resurrection, whilst being pleasing to God, is frequently detested by men and women, for it speaks of their ultimate destiny. The authentic Christian will be undeterred by the costly nature of true service of Jesus, for they will work out their life before the audience of one – *in the sight of God.*

## Questions

1. How does God see Gospel ministry?
2. How do people see Gospel ministry?

3. What do we learn about the significance of Gospel ministry? Why does this lead to the question at the end of verse 16?

4. What should we expect Gospel ministry to look and feel like?

5. Which aspects of being a slave for the Gospel do you find most difficult?

6. What would you say to someone who was trying to avoid the division of verse 16?

7. How does 'working in the sight of God' encourage you to keep presenting the genuine Gospel?

## Excursus: who is the 'we' in 2 Corinthians?

Paul uses the first person throughout the letter. The first person plural (we) predominates in chapters 1 to 9, and the first person singular (I) in chapters 10-13. But, who is the 'we'? Our answer to this question, in light of the key verse of the letter (chapter 5 verse 12, as outlined in the Introduction – *We are not commending ourselves to you again but giving you cause to boast about us, so that you may be able to answer those who boast about outward appearance and not about what is in the heart*) explains the applications that we have made throughout this book.

There are four different uses:

1. Paul, Timothy and Silvanus. Where specified, *we* includes Timothy, the co-sender of the letter, and Silvanus (1:18-19).

2. Paul as an apostle. In chapter 1 verse 1 Paul describes himself as an apostle of Christ. There are unquestionably aspects of his ministry that are unique to him because of this special appointment. He enjoyed a particular commissioning (2:17), and as one to whom the Gospel was given by God, can describe himself as one 'entrusted with the message of reconciliation' (5:19) and one through whom God is making His appeal (5:20), in a way that those who are not Apostles cannot.

3. Paul as a Gospel servant. On further occasions Paul describes his own ministry in ways that do not include specific references

to his role as an Apostle. There is variation in the extent to which these instances describe all Gospel ministry or are more specifically referring to the Corinthian context cf. 2:14-17; 3:1-6; 4:1-15; 5:11-6:13.

4. Paul as a Christian. On a number of occasions, *we* must refer to all Christians, since it is used to describe circumstances that are true of all members of the new covenant. That is seen in chapter 3 verses 12 to 18, where an exemplary 'one' is cited in 3:16, and then 'we all' in 3:18; in chapter 4 verse 14, where the future resurrection of all believers is referred to; in chapter 4 verse 16 to chapter 5 verse 10, where the experience of 'outer wasting' and 'inner renewal' (4:16) is common to all Christians, along with 'the eternal weight of glory beyond all comparison' (4:17); in chapter 5 verse 18 with reference to the reconciliation of Christ; and in chapter 5 verse 21 with reference to becoming *the righteousness of God*.

Paul recognises that his ministry as an Apostle should 'shape' the ministry of all Gospel servants. He then wants the Corinthians to 'boast' in that kind of ministry, and 'line up' with those who practise it. Therefore, as you and I read 'we' today, we are not firstly thinking about ourselves and our ministry. Rather, we are learning what real ministry looks like, so that we can find it, keep connected to it, and be confident in it. Then, at a secondary level, those of us who are currently engaged in Christian service can learn from Paul what our ministry should look like. On the identified occasions where Paul is referring to all Christians, lines of application can be drawn directly to us today.

# 2

# The Substance of Authentic Christian Ministry

## 2 Corinthians 3:1-18

**3** *¹ Are we beginning to commend ourselves again? Or do we need, as some do, letters of recommendation to you, or from you? ² You yourselves are our letter of recommendation, written on our hearts, to be known and read by all. ³ And you show that you are a letter from Christ delivered by us, written not with ink but with the Spirit of the living God, not on tablets of stone but on tablets of human hearts.*

*⁴ Such is the confidence that we have through Christ toward God. ⁵ Not that we are sufficient in ourselves to claim anything as coming from us, but our sufficiency is from God, ⁶ who has made us competent to be ministers of a new covenant, not of the letter but of the Spirit. For the letter kills, but the Spirit gives life.*

*⁷ Now if the ministry of death, carved in letters on stone, came with such glory that the Israelites could not gaze at Moses' face because of its glory, which was being brought to an end, ⁸ will not the ministry of the Spirit have even more glory? ⁹ For if there was glory in the ministry of condemnation, the ministry of righteousness must far exceed it in glory. ¹⁰ Indeed, in this case, what once had glory has come to have no glory at all, because of the* *glory that surpasses it. <sup>11</sup>For if what was being brought to an end came with glory, much more will what is permanent have glory.*

*<sup>12</sup>Since we have such a hope, we are very bold, <sup>13</sup>not like Moses, who would put a veil over his face so that the Israelites might not gaze at the outcome of what was being brought to an end. <sup>14</sup>But their minds were hardened. For to this day, when they read the old covenant, that same veil remains unlifted, because only through Christ is it taken away. <sup>15</sup>Yes, to this day whenever Moses is read a veil lies over their hearts. <sup>16</sup>But when one turns to the Lord, the veil is removed. <sup>17</sup>Now the Lord is the Spirit, and where the Spirit of the Lord is, there is freedom. <sup>18</sup>And we all, with unveiled face, beholding the glory of the Lord, are being transformed into the same image from one degree of glory to another. For this comes from the Lord who is the Spirit.*

2 CORINTHIANS chapter three is the theological heart of the letter. Here Paul spells out the content of authentic Christian ministry, defining its substance. The chapter divides into four parts.

## 1. Transformation (vv. 1 to 3 and v. 18)

As Paul commends himself from chapter 2 verse 16b to chapter 3 verse 3, he holds up his qualification for the task. Notice the concern in these verses for the adequacy, sufficiency and qualification for ministry.

Paul holds up the lives of the Corinthian Christians as exhibits demonstrating his Gospel ministry to be authentic. It is clear that he has something public in mind, when he says the Corinthians are *to be known and read by all*. His expectation of authentic Christian ministry is that whilst being a work on the inside, *in the heart* (5:12), it nonetheless produces radical external change, noticeable to all. Hence he writes here that the Corinthians are *to be known and read by all*. This idea is picked up in chapter 3 verse 18, where Paul says:

*And we all, with unveiled face, beholding the glory of the Lord, are being transformed into the same image from one degree of glory to another.*

Furthermore, the verses make clear that real change is taking place in the present: *are being transformed.* It is not something way off in the future. God brings this genuine change. It is transformation that happens to us, and is not something that we produce ourselves. The verb in verse 18 is passive, 'are *being* transformed'. We see this same expectation of change elsewhere in the letter. In chapter 7, Paul speaks of his joy at their repentance. In chapter 12 verse 20 Paul fears he will not find the Corinthians as he wishes. In chapter 13 verse 7 Paul speaks about coming to test them, and the test is whether there has been real restoration. Paul's concern, then, is that what has happened authentically on the inside is matched by something genuine on the outside.

But notice how this change comes in verse 3. Paul's language suggests that he understands himself to be playing the role of postman. Paul sees himself as delivering the Corinthians as his 'letter of recommendation'. They are a letter *from* Christ, written *by* the Holy Spirit. This immediately poses a major challenge to the false teachers. They were clearly men of the Jewish Law, being described in chapter 11 as Hebrews, Israelites and offspring of Abraham. They were super-spiritual men who boasted of their experiences. They were expecting the change to be brought about through the Old Testament covenant, which Moses wrote on tablets of stone. Paul rejects this. Instead he tells us that real Christian change comes from an authentic work of the Spirit, in the heart of an individual.

A careful reading of the whole letter enables something of a pen-portrait of these false leaders to be constructed. Clearly these *peddlers of God's Word* (2:17) were religious and saw Moses and the Old Covenant as key. It seems that they sought accreditation for their ministry through the religious and ritualistic conduct of their followers. We might say they were 'super-religious'.

In addition, we learn of their boasting about spiritual experience and oratorical skills. They sought accreditation for their ministry through so-called experiences of the Spirit (5:12-13 connect the erroneous boasting in outward appearances with the ecstatic experience of being 'beside yourself'.) They were offering a different spirit to the Corinthians than the Spirit that the Corinthians had first received (11:4). Paul presents himself as being in no way inferior to the peddlers in their experiences (5:13 *if we are beside ourselves*; 12:1 *I will go on to visions and revelations of the Lord;* 12:4 *he heard things that cannot be told, which man may not utter),* but he refuses to use these experiences to commend his ministry. We might say that these peddlers were 'super-spiritual'.

Furthermore, in chapter 10 verse 10 and chapter 11 verse 6, we read that perceived oratorical skills were of great importance to them. We might say that they were 'super-slick'. Paul's argument, however, is that true Gospel ministry is a work of God, in which God has brought real change in the heart of a believer, resulting in genuine transformation. First and foremost, it is not about surface activity. It is a heart matter. Only a changed heart can produce a changed life.

Throughout the history of the church, similar 'peddlers' have emerged claiming authenticity through 'on the face' experiences. (In 5:12, 'on the face' is presented as being the undesirable opposite of true ministry, which brings change 'on the heart'. 'On the face' is our literal translation. The ESV translates the phrase as 'outward appearance'.) The Toronto Blessing back in the 1990s was such a movement. People falling over, barking like dogs and collapsing in hysterics were claimed to be signs of God's work. It was a real 'on the face', surface-level ministry. One senior Christian leader, when asked about the Toronto Blessing, responded, 'It's not so much what they do when they fall over that I'm concerned about, it's what they do when they stand up.' Authentic Christian ministry will produce radical change.

'On the face' ministries are deeply appealing, because they seem to offer a quick and effective solution to any problems and challenges that a ministry experiences. Paul wants the Corinthians to be more discerning. When considering whether a ministry is genuine, there are a number of things not to be bothered about: attendance at services, the number of people in small-group bible studies, and the oratorical skill of the speaker. The key questions of authenticity are: 'is this the genuine message?' and 'is there real change?' So, says Paul, if you want to know whether there is a genuine ministry, look at: their marriages, their language, how they have controlled their tongue, the way they love each other, how they spend their money, their sexual relationships, the way they treat their colleagues, the way children are cared for when they come into their community and the way they care for their elderly. Is there radical transformation?

Those who have been Christians for a significant length of time may be at risk of not expecting this ministry of transformation to be happening to them anymore, whether from the pulpit, in small groups, or in personal Bible reading. Perhaps it did in the past, but there is no longer that personal expectation and confidence. But Paul knows no such limitations! Transformation is expected to be an ongoing process until glory. There is the very great danger that people will try and create some new 'on the face' or 'silver bullet' solution to see this transformation happen quickly and visibly. But there are no shortcuts. The rest of this chapter shows us how this heart-change happens.

## 2.  Regeneration (vv. 4 to 6)

Verses 1 to 3 raise the issue and spell out the evidence of real change, and we must keep reading to learn how this heart-changing transformation occurs. Verses 4 to 6 show us that a miraculous, supernatural work of God has taken place.

Paul's repeated use of the Greek word translated as 'sufficient' is striking (twice in verse 5 and once in verse 6, where it is translated as 'competent'). The sufficiency that Paul is pointing to is from God. It is God who brings the believer alive, by the work of His Holy Spirit. Paul is again using the language of life, death and sufficiency also seen in chapter 2 verses 15 to 16. He sees himself in weakness, at the back of the triumphal procession. Yet as he speaks the Gospel, so God brings life. This work of God is a key idea throughout the early chapters of the letter. It is found here in chapter 3 verse 6, *the Spirit gives life*. It is also seen in chapter 4 verse 6: *For God, who said, 'Let light shine out of darkness', has shone in our hearts*, and in chapter 5 verse 17, *Therefore, if anyone is in Christ, he is a new creation.*

Under the Old Covenant, before the coming of Christ, there could be no bringing of spiritual life to a person's heart. However, the regenerative work of Christ now brings this radical change. God the Father, through the work of God the Son, by the power of God the Holy Spirit, brings life. The change on the outside does not come through the ascetic rigour of rules, regulations and rituals; nor through the surface froth of super-spiritual experience or slick presentation. Instead it comes from a radical new beginning in the heart of a person. This is seen both in verse 3: *not on tablets of stone but on tablets of human hearts*, and at the end of verse 6: *For the letter kills, but the Spirit gives life.* This is real Christian work, done by Father, Son and Holy Spirit in peoples' hearts. This work is often referred to as the doctrine of Regeneration, which means bringing new life. A person who is regenerate is no longer dead on the inside, but has been made alive.

This teaching is once again a direct assault on the false teachers. They were clearly Jewish (see 11:22) and they wanted to bind people into the Old Testament law, the Ten Commandments and what is called the Old Covenant. But from Genesis 3 onwards, having rebelled against God, all human beings are dead on the inside. *The wages of sin is death* (Rom. 6:23), and the hearts of all people are dead on the inside, because everyone has rebelled against God. All people are cut-off from God, and are without the life of God on the inside. There is no flicker of life within. The Old Testament consistently points forward to the day when God would do a radical new work. He would change the hearts of His people, by washing them clean and flooding His Holy Spirit into them, by bringing life. The promise in Ezekiel chapter 36 verses 25 to 27 demonstrates this:

> *I will sprinkle clean water on you, and you shall be clean from all your uncleannesses, and from all your idols I will cleanse you. And I will give you a new heart, and a new spirit I will put within you. And I will remove the heart of stone from your flesh and give you a heart of flesh. And I will put my Spirit within you, and cause you to walk in my statutes and be careful to obey my rules.*

The ministry that is on the outside can wag its finger at you and tell you to pull your moral socks up. But that is something that people who are dead on the inside cannot achieve. The ministry that is only froth, glamour and excitement in the big public hall, where people are falling over and people are merely showing off their clever oratorical skills, cannot bring life. Human beings cannot bring life to dead hearts. Paul says that he is qualified, confident and sufficient, because he is speaking about a ministry performed by God the Father, God the Son, and God the Holy Spirit, on the inside. It is performed on the heart of the unbeliever, on what is otherwise a dead, calcified heart of stone. Here is the essence of true Christian ministry.

So this radical transformation that Paul describes does not come from trying harder or shouting louder, or by becoming more extreme.

Nor does it come from more rules and regulations, or from more pull-ups and push-ups in the spiritual gym. Authentic change comes through a genuine work of the Holy Spirit as He brings new life into the heart of the believer. At the centre of authentic Gospel ministry is spiritual surgery. God is in the business of heart transplants. When a person becomes a Christian, something goes on quietly, secretly, in their inner being, as God creates a new heart within them. You may not quite remember when it happened to you, or you might be able to name the day. Praise God that He did this work in me on December 18th 1979! God has done this miracle of heart surgery in every Christian, through the Gospel. God does not make physical incisions into us; instead His work happens through the proclamation of Jesus Christ. Paul has undertaken this task of proclamation without needing any special qualifications, or letters of recommendation. The Corinthian Christians were his evidence that through hearing the Gospel, Father, Son and Holy Spirit had worked a miracle. This work is the concern of every true church.

## 3. Justification (vv. 7 to 11)

The question of how this Regeneration actually happens must then be considered. We have seen Transformation, happening through Regeneration. Wider Christian circles can suggest various possibilities: that Regeneration is something magical and mystical; that it comes through the sacraments; that it is connected to a particular experience of the Holy Spirit; that it can come through doing a particular course. It is hugely important to be clear on how Regeneration happens, because chapter 11 has shown us that it is possible to proclaim a different Jesus, a different Spirit, and a different gospel. There are plenty of people *peddling* God's Word. Paul answers this question in chapter 3 verses 7 to 11. He shows us that the ministry of Transformation comes through the work of Regeneration, which God brings about through the Justification of the believer.

Verses 7 to 11 compare and contrast two glorious ministries. But one is quite definitely more glorious than the other! By way of background, the *letters on stone* are talking about the Law of Moses. The *ministry of condemnation* is referring to Old Covenant ministry. As Moses came down the mountain in Exodus 34, his face was ablaze, because he had been speaking with God Himself. It was a glorious ministry. But the Gospel ministry that 2 Corinthians lays out for us is so much more spectacular, that the Old Covenant ministry now no longer seems to shine at all.

This is in no way to downplay the ministry of the Old Covenant. Paul describes it as glorious! It is glorious in its moral perfection. The Ten Commandments are glorious. Just one of them: *you shall not commit adultery*, is a glorious thing. Cultures in which this commandment is treated lightly then quickly experience moral and social disintegration, and head back into the cultural dark ages. *You shall not murder. You shall not covet.* These are also glorious commandments. *You shall love the LORD your God with all your heart, mind, soul and strength.* It is a glorious reality to have one unifying truth of a Creator God, to whom we can submit ourselves!

The ministry of Moses is glorious in its moral perfection. But it is also glorious in its justice. In Exodus chapter 34 verse 7 God declares that He *will by no means clear the guilty.* God shows Himself to be a just judge. He will not brush things under the carpet, or pretend that things have never happened. He sees everything. He knows everything. He will judge everything. And He will not acquit the guilty.

The idea of the guilty getting away with it greatly concerns us as a culture, and new investigations are regularly launched. Paedophile scandals, hospital care and FIFA are among the areas and institutions under scrutiny at the time of writing. Time may forget some of these examples, but our culture hates injustice so much that a quick glance at the news headlines will likely deliver several alternative cases. There are no such fears of injustice with God.

The ministry of the Old Covenant is glorious, because the Covenant has both moral and judicial perfection. However, this leads Paul to describe the ministry of the Old Covenant as a ministry of death, and condemnation. Condemnation, because as the Ten Commandments are held up, our guilt is undeniable. The person who thinks that they have never murdered anyone, then hears the teaching of Jesus in Matthew 5: *You have heard that it was said to those of old, 'You shall not murder; and whoever murders will be liable to judgment.' But I say to you that everyone who is angry with his brother will be liable to judgment (vv. 21 and 22)*. The Law condemns us. We are murderers. *Everyone who looks at a woman with lustful intent has already committed adultery with her in his heart (v. 28)*. The Law condemns us. We are adulterers. There are things which we have done that we should not have. There are also things which we should have done, which we have not. And the most important commandment says, *you shall love the Lord your God with all your heart and with all your soul and with all your mind and with all your strength* (Mark 12:30). The worst sin, then, is *not* to love the Lord with all my heart, all my soul, all my mind and all my strength. No-one can say that they have done that. Even today – *all* your mind, *all* your heart, *all* your strength? The Law condemns us. We have committed the worst sin in the book. And worse than that, because God is a God of perfect justice (and thank God that He is!), we face the penalty, and *the wages of sin is death* (Rom. 6:23). And so this glorious ministry of the Old Covenant, of the Law, of moral and judicial perfection, is a ministry of death and condemnation.

All religion leaves people dead and condemned. That is the case whether it is Islam and the five pillars, or Hinduism, or something else. No human religion enables us to meet God's moral and judicial perfection. Above all, that is true for the glorious ministry delivered by God, apart from Jesus. Our culture has abandoned the first four commandments, and has tailored the second six to suit our own bankrupt and compromised morality. But God *will by no means aquit the guilty* (Exod. 34:7).

The word translated *righteousness* in verse 9 is the same word as that used for 'justification'. They come from the same root in Greek. It is the language of the court room, and means 'to declare to be right'. The Spirit of God, because of the finished work of the Son of God, Jesus, on the cross, brings to the heart of the believer the status of being justified. When someone is justified, they are declared to be in the right. It is not solely a declaration that they have done nothing wrong. As we have seen, God's Law demands that people do lots of things right. When someone is justified, they are credited with and are given, the perfect life that Jesus Christ lived. The life visible on the pages of the Gospels, is reckoned to us. Jesus is the only one who has always loved God with all His heart, soul, mind and strength. Jesus is the only one who has never murdered, or committed adultery. And justification counts that perfect life, to me. As one preacher helpfully put it, 'Did you know that because of the finished work of Jesus on the cross, if you trust in Jesus, God sees you today as perfect?'

This is the doctrine of Justification. There is nothing more exciting! It is important to be clear that whilst this work is achieved at the cross through the substitutionary sacrificial death of Jesus, it is applied to the believer's heart by the Holy Spirit. Thus, at the core of the marvellous, miraculous, majestic work of God the Holy Spirit, is this work of bringing to a believer the righteous, justified status. Those who look for the 'on the face' and at 'outward appearance' are always looking for something human, that seems more important, or more wonderful than Justification.

On one occasion a Christian minister preached on the cross, and there was a man in the congregation who was looking for something 'on the face', a different sort of ministry. It was a fantastic talk. On being asked what he thought of the sermon, the man replied, 'Oh, I prefer something more spiritual.' His comment showed that he did not have the first idea about the ministry of the Spirit. He had completely missed the point. There can be nothing more spiritual, more supernatural, more marvellous, or more magnificent than God the Holy Spirit bringing Regeneration to bear in the life of a believer, through declaring the Justification that God achieves in the heart of a believer, through the finished work of Jesus on the cross.

Some people find greatest spiritual excitement in being served by impressive people in particular clothes performing routines and rituals. Such a preference, over hearing the Gospel and seeing that work of Regeneration, shows that they have not understood the Christian Gospel properly. They are thinking like the Corinthians in this letter. The Apostle Paul would say, *but I am afraid that as the serpent deceived Eve by his cunning, your thoughts will be led astray from a sincere and pure devotion to Christ. For if someone comes and proclaims another Jesus than the one we proclaimed, or if you receive a different spirit from the one you received, or if you accept a different gospel from the one you accepted, you put up with it readily enough.* (11:3-4).

## 4. Illumination (vv. 12 to 18)

The doctrine of Illumination is the subject of verses 12 to 18 (although the word itself does not appear here). It is only the Holy Spirit who can open our hearts and minds to the glorious truth about Jesus Christ.

The word translated 'bold' in verse 12 refers particularly to bold and courageous speech. Since Paul understands that Gospel proclamation is the means by which God changes human hearts, he is therefore 'bold *to speak*'. However he might have felt, he declared the Gospel to people. Paul was not like Moses, who put a veil over his face so that the Israelites might not gaze at the outcome of what was being brought to an end.

Paul once again takes us to Moses, because in Corinth the Jewish false teachers were infatuated with the Old Testament. When Moses came down from the mountain in Exodus 34, his face was ablaze. He had been speaking face to face with the living God, and he covered his face from the Israelites until he went in to speak with God again. They could not see the glory of Moses' ministry, or the temporary, fading nature of it. Paul then speaks of a figurative veil, which prevents the recipients of Old Covenant ministry from 'beholding the glory of the Lord'. Old Covenant ministry can do nothing to overcome the 'hardened minds' and 'covered hearts' of people who read the Law. But now, in and through Jesus, we can *behold the glory of the Lord* (v. 18).

Exodus 34 tells us that the Israelites were utterly terrified when they saw Moses, a truly godly person, after he had just met face to face with God. Now however, the Christian, who has been justified, does not need to be frightened of God. Since Jesus has brought this justification to the heart, the Christian can now gaze on the glory of God, in the face of Christ. They can actually look on God without fear of condemnation and death. The veil has been removed. It is a truly remarkable thing. So as the Christian looks on Jesus, and sees a life of *love, joy, peace, patience, kindness, goodness, faithfulness, gentleness and self-control* (Gal. 5:22), their new heart is instructed, fed and illumined. And so they are being transformed. God the Holy Spirit is on the inside, working out transformation, as they gaze on the truth of Christ. However, in the Corinthian context, it must be remembered that a 'transformed' Christian will not look impressive in the world's eyes.

Looking at the sun via a mirror illustrates this pattern. Someone can gaze at the sun by using a mirror. And simultaneously, the glory of the sun reflects back on them by way of the mirror, and they are lit up. Similarly, the glory of God has been made known to us in the person of Christ. Christians have now been made free to gaze on Him, as the veil has been taken away, and they are not condemned. As they gaze on Christ, the Spirit is lighting up their heart. They are being transformed from one degree of glory into another. It is a slow work. It is a painfully difficult work. But it is a work that is not happening through an 'on the surface' razzmatazz. It is happening as the heart is Regenerated, through the Justification of Christ, and as the Justified come to the Scriptures and gaze on the person of Jesus.

## Conclusion

2 Corinthians chapter 3 shows us the theological heart of real Christian ministry. Through such ministry, the Holy Spirit brings real Transformation and change. The contrast is made with false ministries which only bring change on the surface. Such Transformation can only happen when God Regenerates a person's heart, bringing them from death to life. It is Justification that enables this Regeneration – the Spirit of God applying Christ's finished work on the cross to the heart, so that the Christian is declared to be in the right before God. The Holy Spirit then keeps opening the heart and mind to the glorious truth about Jesus. This is Illumination, which in turn brings Transformation.

The chapter's consistent contrast with Moses and Old Covenant ministry shows that there is a choice to be made. Moses' was a ministry that looked outwardly impressive, but was unable to change the heart. There are *peddlers of God's Word* today who are only concerned with how things look on the outside. By exposing the shallowness of such ministries, and showing us the lasting glory of genuine Gospel ministry, Paul is urging us to keep our confidence in this New Covenant ministry.

## Questions

1. Using the ideas of these verses, write a sentence of not more than 50 words that explains why the Christian Gospel and Gospel ministry is 'glorious' despite appearances.

2. How has what Paul tells us of the Gospel here encouraged you, personally?

3. In what ways does Paul's teaching in these verses give you confidence to be 'very bold' (v. 12) in speaking the Gospel to people you know who are not Christians?

4. How does what Paul says here about the Gospel change what you think both about the Gospel and the nature of true Gospel ministry?

5. In what ways does this passage encourage those who might be feeling worn-down in Christian ministry, and challenge those who are contemplating moving to something that looks more impressive?

The big ideas that we have seen in this chapter are illustrated and summarised in this diagram:

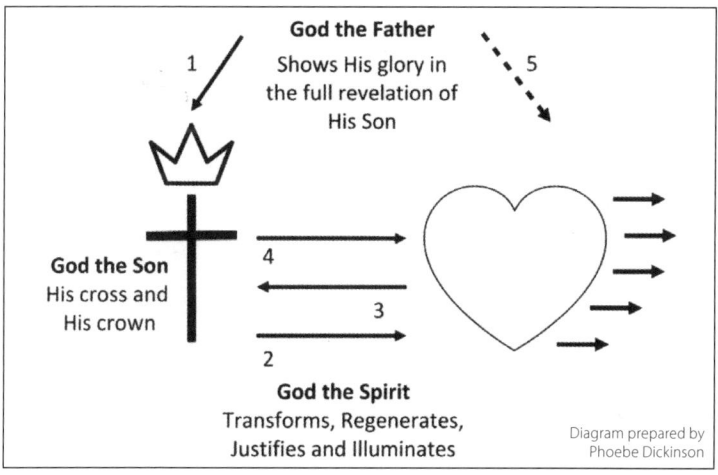

**God the Father**
Shows His glory in the full revelation of His Son

1

5

**God the Son**
His cross and His crown

4

3

2

**God the Spirit**
Transforms, Regenerates, Justifies and Illuminates

Diagram prepared by
Phoebe Dickinson

**1.** God the Father has made His glory known, in an historical, public act of revelation, in God the Son, for all to see. This glory is seen in the full revelation of the Son: in His cross, His crown and kingship, His death, His resurrection, and His enthroning in heaven. Therefore, relying on Moses to see the glory of God, as the Israelites did, is no longer the way. God the Father can now be seen in Jesus Christ and the public revelation in the Scriptures. This revelation was a mystery, but it has now been made known.

**2.** God the Holy Spirit takes this public truth, of the possibility of Regeneration through Justification, and writes it on the heart of the believer. Therefore Paul's ministry, though not a ministry of dazzling tricks, is of immense supernatural power, because it is written in the heart. Therefore Paul wants us to boast in the ministry that impacts the heart, rather than in ministries that just produce surface change.

**3.** But now, the one whose heart has been cleansed by the Holy Spirit and His power, by the power of the Spirit is able to gaze back on the glory of God in the face of Christ without fear. The people of Moses' day could not do this. As this is done, the glory of God can be witnessed in His revelation of Jesus Christ.

**4.** As these things are seen, and as the Jesus of history in the pages of Scripture is contemplated, considered, meditated on and thought about, so the Holy Spirit moves in the heart to bring Transformation. The Christian is being transformed from one degree of glory to another.

Notice how God-centred this is. Talk of transforming the heart is popular today. The key point to remember is that heart-transformation is entirely a work of God, and is therefore not man-centred. God removes the veil, God reveals Himself, God brings a person alive, and God enables a person to gaze on His glory in the face of Christ. And as the glory of God in the face of Christ is gazed on, God brings conviction of sin, and produces Transformation – love, joy, peace, patience, kindness, goodness, faithfulness, gentleness, and self-control.

The key to Transformation from a human point of view is deliberate and dependent meditation on the Scriptures. Such activity anticipates that God will bring Transformation by the power of His Holy Spirit who is living within us. Transformation does not come by following rules and regulations. Nor does it come by following religious rituals, through attending glamorous meetings, or through reading glossy magazines about the Christian life. Rather, Transformation comes through the quiet, unseen ministry of word and prayer, in the power of the Holy Spirit, which produces change in the heart.

**5.** Do not believe any Bible teacher who says that God the Father works direct through God the Spirit, into the heart. Such teaching is Binitarian theology, not Trinitarian theology. All over the world, and in many different forms of so called Christianity, this theology appears. It looks exciting, but it is surface religion, 'on the face'. It is not true Christianity, which is Christ-ianity. Paul insists that a genuine work of God the Holy Spirit is radically focused on Jesus. Perhaps such ministry does not initially look quite so exciting, but the long-term results are much more impressive.

# 3

# The Motivations of Authentic Christian Ministry

## 2 Corinthians 4:1-6

*¹Therefore, having this ministry by the mercy of God, we do not lose heart. ²But we have renounced disgraceful, underhanded ways. We refuse to practice cunning or to tamper with God's word, but by the open statement of the truth we would commend ourselves to everyone's conscience in the sight of God. ³And even if our gospel is veiled, it is veiled to those who are perishing. ⁴In their case the god of this world has blinded the minds of the unbelievers, to keep them from seeing the light of the gospel of the glory of Christ, who is the image of God. ⁵For what we proclaim is not ourselves, but Jesus Christ as Lord, with ourselves as your servants for Jesus' sake. ⁶For God, who said, 'Let light shine out of darkness,' has shone in our hearts to give the light of the knowledge of the glory of God in the face of Jesus Christ.*

THE issue Paul turns to in Chapter 4 is that of losing heart or growing weary. This can be seen from chapter 4 verse 1, where the phrase *we do not lose heart* carries the sense of growing weary, or being discouraged, while doing a good thing. The same idea can also be found in chapter 4 verse 16, *we do not lose heart*. It is put positively in chapter 3 verse 12, *we are very bold* and chapter 5 verse 6, *we are always of good courage.*

This is the section of the letter where Paul is arguing in support of his ministry. The reason he is doing this, from chapter 5 verse 12, is because he wants us to boast in it. Paul's point is that he wants us not just to side with him, but to be engaged in this kind of ministry in our churches. Paul wants to recruit us, or keep us, in authentic Gospel ministry.

The idea of losing heart is a familiar one. We speak of people 'throwing in the towel'. Phrases like 'he's lost the will to live', 'she's given up on him', 'he's had enough', and 'she's chucked it in' are commonplace in the sporting world, the workplace and the church.

A brief survey of the Corinthian letters shows Paul providing at least five reasons that can easily cause us to lose heart. Such examples are all the more striking when contrasted with the previous chapter, which speaks of the glory of true Gospel ministry.

## Plans are frustrated

Though often hailed as the great church planter, the New Testament shows that Paul's plans were regularly frustrated and turned on their head. In Damascus, his death was plotted, so he escaped by night (Acts 9:1-25, recounted in 2 Corinthians 11:32-33). Paul was sent away from both Thessalonica and Berea (Acts 17: 10, 14) because of opposition against him. From the start of 2 Corinthians we discover that Paul's plans to visit Corinth have been frustrated (1:15-17). People often have great hopes and ambitions in Christian ministry, but then perhaps five years down the track, plans have been frustrated, and it may look as though not very much has been achieved at all.

## People are frustrating

For those who have been engaged in Christian ministry for any length of time, it will not be difficult to draw up a list of people to whom hours of time have been committed, but who never seem to have made any progress at all, maybe in their investigation of the Gospel, or in their Christian lives. Perhaps it was a weekly one-to-one Bible study over a number of years with a person who is now opposed to Christ. Perhaps consistent time praying for people over decades, who are now no nearer to Christian belief. Perhaps the reason people draw back or fall away like this is because Paul's preaching demanded real change. The Christian Gospel requires repentance. Paul writes of his *painful visit* in chapter 2 verse 1 and of a letter written *out of much affliction and anguish of heart and with many tears* (2:4). It can be uncomfortable calling for repentance, and people will leave churches where repentance is required. It would be easy for the Gospel worker to lose heart! Similarly, it would be easy for others in the congregation to lose heart, as they wonder why their minister seems unable to positively influence some people. Paul fears that he himself may face a similar frustration with the Corinthians. In chapter 12 verse 20 he says, *I fear that perhaps when I come I may not find you as I wish.* The reason for that fear is *that perhaps there may be quarrelling, jealousy, anger, hostility, slander, gossip, conceit, and disorder* among them.

## Proclamation seems futile

Gospel proclamation is ultimately an unseen ministry. This will be explored further in the consideration of chapter 5 of the letter. There are times when the preacher has given his all, presenting such vital eternal realities as judgment and forgiveness, heaven and hell, eternal life and eternal separation from God. Then after the service he finds people completely unmoved and wanting to talk about anything apart from what they have heard. They seem more interested in football than eternal life! Proclamation can seem so futile when people show little hunger for the Gospel message that has been expounded.

## Opposition is fierce

In 2 Corinthians 10 Paul speaks of strongholds of disobedience to Christ. With respect to these, Paul says, *We destroy arguments and every lofty opinion raised against the knowledge of God* (10:5). Opposition to the Gospel is fierce and intense whatever the location; whether labouring for Christ in the town or the country, it can sometimes feel like the heart of Babylon. Christian workers often feel like turning right round, and going back the other way.

## Personal failings are obvious

Paul felt weak, and his ministry looked unimpressive. He talks of *some who suspect us of walking according to the flesh* (10:2), that some think *his bodily presence is weak, and his speech of no account* (10:10), others that he is *unskilled in speaking* (11:6). Additionally, he says that *a thorn was given me in the flesh* (12:7). To be conscious of one's own failures and inadequacies is the normal experience of Christian ministry, and it leads us to ask with Paul, *who is sufficient for these things?* (2:16).

This is then the issue, and Paul's aim in writing is that we do not give up. There are five reasons in six verses which suggest why we should persevere. Paul has structured these verses like a sandwich: verses 1 and 6 match each other; as do verses 2 and 5, and 3 and 4.

We do not give up, because:

## 1.  The Commission is God-given (v. 1)

Paul says in verse 1 that *by the mercy of God*, he has been entrusted with the ministry described in chapter 3. It is the ministry of Gospel proclamation. It is the glorious ministry of the Spirit who, through the proclamation of Jesus and His New Covenant, brings justification to the heart of the believer. Once justified, the Spirit then enables the Christian to gaze on Christ through His Word, and so be transformed from one degree of glory to another. Therefore, how could Paul ever lose heart? This ministry, with which he has been entrusted, is the glorious ministry of the Spirit. It is the ministry that brings regeneration, creating new life. It is the ministry that brings justification. This ministry has the power to change hearts. It is more glorious than the ministry of Moses.

Most people have been 'commissioned' for a job at some stage, whether after finishing school, on leaving university, or trying to find casual work. The skills needed for some jobs can be picked up quite quickly. Others, such as surgery and architecture, need years and years of training. Our culture attaches great significance to jobs, and the training needed for them. And yet here Paul says that he, as a Christian preacher, has the greatest job in the world, given to him by God. God has commissioned Paul for a ministry that changes hearts. It is a ministry given only by His mercy, and that is not earned. The commission is from God. Therefore, we do not lose heart.

## 2. The method is straight talk (vv. 2 and 5a)

Verse 2, in combination with the first half of verse 5, is absolutely key. It shows us what real Christian ministry is, according to the Apostle Paul. The first half of the verse 2 focuses on the negative, on Dodgy Dealing. The second half focuses on the positive, laying out the Professional Standards of the Gospel servant.

### Dodgy Dealing

*Disgraceful, underhanded ways* (literally 'secret and shameful') calls to mind the false teachers of 2 Corinthians, who were seeking to infiltrate and redirect the church. Paul has described them as carrying *letters of recommendation* (3:1), and later he will show us that they *measure themselves by one another and compare themselves with one another* (10:12), and he accuses them of being *false apostles, deceitful workmen, disguising themselves as apostles of Christ* (11:13). They work in disguise. They take advantage of people. They puff themselves up. They commend each other. They compare themselves with each other. They boast about their ministry. They peddle the Word. They are self-promoting, self-seeking, and self-advancing.

There is therefore a style of Christian ministry that is 'disgraceful and underhanded'. As Christians we can be far too undiscerning about this. When exposed to this sort of ministry, we can all too easily assume that because a teacher is calling himself a Christian, and using Jesus' name, and speaking about the Spirit, therefore he must be reliable. However, from chapter 11 we know that the false teachers did preach Jesus, but a different Jesus. They did speak of the Holy Spirit, but a different Spirit. They did do gospel work, but a different gospel work. They called themselves Christians: Paul calls them *disgraceful, underhanded.*

Verse 2 then shows two characteristics of the method used by such 'peddlers'. They are Deceptive, performing tricks with the message. They are Distorting, tampering with the message.

### We refuse to practise cunning

The word behind deceit, cunning, and trickery literally means 'to refuse to do anything'. It is the philosophy of 'it doesn't matter how you do it – just get the client!' Or, 'it doesn't matter what it takes – just seal the deal.' Paul says he refuses to 'do anything'. Gospel servants should not perform tricks with the message. Cunning and trickery are the tactics of *The Apprentice*, unleashed in the church.

Such tricks are a particular temptation when we understand that the stakes are so high. We want the Gospel to advance. We do not want our friends to perish. We long for the glory of God to be known. There is therefore a danger of dressing-up the message or perhaps dressing-up the meeting. Our celebrity age is all style and no substance. How easy it is to seek to attract a crowd, and to look impressive. The lights might be turned down, and the music turned up. The 'beautiful people' might deliberately be put up front, we might seek to appoint preachers who are little more than entertainers. But Paul wants to know whether the ministry is being done in a disgraceful and underhanded way.

We will not perform tricks with the message, but also:

### *We refuse to tamper with God's Word*

God has delivered, once for all, a message that changes hearts, by His Spirit, through His Word. So Gospel ministers are not at liberty to play around with the message. The Greek word translated here as 'practise cunning' is that for bait in a snare. Paul does not try and snare people.

Most heresies in the modern church have come about because people have wanted to draw others in. David Jenkins, the former Bishop of Durham who denied the physical resurrection of Jesus, did so primarily to try and make the Christian Gospel seem more credible in a scientific age. For 'the best of reasons', he pursued his line that the idea of a physical resurrection was thought to be unbelievable to the modern world, and that the resurrection was simply a spiritual thing and not a physical raising of the dead body of Jesus. Similarly, those in the Church of England and other mainline denominations who are seeking to change the churches' stance on sexual ethics are doing so in large part in order to make the Christian faith more appealing to the world. Other movements downplay Jesus' teaching on judgment, God's wrath and hell, for what they consider to be evangelistic purposes. Paul says that we should refuse to tamper with God's Word.

## Professional Standards

Paul uses the word for 'shining a light' as he describes his ministry of laying out the truth, plainly. The need for the open statement of the truth raises the question of what the truth actually is. Verse 5 provides the answer.

### *About God*

The truth which Paul openly states is that Jesus Christ is Lord – *what we proclaim is not ourselves, but Jesus Christ as Lord.*

It must be noted that this is a verbal task. This God-given commission is to speak the Christian Gospel. Powerful, authentic Gospel ministry is proclaiming that Jesus Christ is Lord. The content of Paul's Gospel should also be noticed: Jesus Christ – the Jesus of history; the Jesus who is Lord of everything. He is not just Lord for a tiny little hour on a Sunday, but is Lord of everything, all the time. And this Jesus demands our submission and repentance.

This is an immensely important verse. From observation, people who lose heart do not usually stop going to church. Instead, they will usually pick a church that in one way or another tempers or tampers with God's Word. Maybe a church that does not talk about sin, or does not say that those who do not believe in Christ are going to hell. Maybe the reality of God's judgment is ignored, or it is a church that does not take the Bible quite so seriously.

Those considering joining a new ministry should seek to discern whether tricks are being performed with the message, whether God's Word is being tampered with, whether absolutely anything will be done to encourage people to join, or whether the truth is simply being taught, plainly and openly.

### *In the sight of God*

Although Paul is writing this letter to a Corinthian audience, and although he preaches to people wherever he goes, his work is ultimately *in the sight of God*, and his primary concern is to please Him. The aim of Gospel servants is not primarily to please those to whom they are ministering. Nor is it to convince themselves that they have done a good job. Rather, Gospel servants are working in the sight of God.

As those served, we often wish our priorities to be the first concern. This might come in the form of favouring some projects over others, or having clear ideas about whom the minister should be spending time with. However, we are reminded here that as those ministered to, we are not the primary audience. Furthermore, we must be able to be confidently and wholeheartedly engaged in a ministry where our approval is demonstrably not the ultimate goal.

On his retirement, one Christian leader was asked by several people whether there were things which he regretted that he had not done. He said, 'There were many things that I did not do, but I never stepped into the pulpit unprepared.' He was totally committed to the open statement of the truth, in the sight of God.

## 3. The results are out of our hands (vv. 3 to 4)

The idea of the results of Gospel ministry being out of our hands is immensely significant. There is a danger that we see someone's failure to sit eagerly and hungrily under God's Word as something that we are responsible for. That may be the case, if a person has not prayerfully worked hard at the plain statement of the truth. But Paul says that if someone fails to respond to his plain statement of God's truth, then it is because their mind is blinded by Satan.

This spiritual perspective of a devil actively at work in Twenty-First Century Western Secularism must be understood. If it is not, motivation for speaking the Gospel will quickly be lost. Again and again people say, 'it's my fault', or think that there is something the matter with this kind of ministry, or with the message, or with the preacher, or with Paul. But Paul says, 'no', the results are out of our hands. The job of the Christian servant is simply to make the message plain.

There are two ways in which the devil's work is seen in 2 Corinthians: blinding – *the god of this world has blinded the minds of the unbelievers* (4:4); and deceiving – *but I am afraid that as the serpent deceived Eve by his cunning, your thoughts will be led astray from a sincere and pure devotion to Christ* (11:3). C.S. Lewis captures these two types of Satan's work so well in *The Screwtape Letters:*

> 'My Dear Wormwood,' says the senior devil, Screwtape, to his accomplice Wormwood, 'I wonder you should ask me whether it is essential to keep the patient in ignorance of your own existence…. The fact that "devils" are predominantly *comic* figures in the modern imagination will help you. If any faint suspicion of your existence begins to arise in his mind, suggest to him a picture of something in red tights.' [1]

I find the truth of verses 3 and 4 of immense importance for the work we do in the Tuesday Lunchtime services at St Helen's. St Helen's is in the middle of the City of London, an area of just one square mile, into which 350,000 people travel every day to work. On any given Tuesday Lunchtime, there are just 250 of us meeting together. At such times, it is easy to wonder whether the Gospel is at all powerful, whether there is anything to the Gospel, and indeed whether this sort of meeting is actually worth doing. Similarly, if the Gospel has been explained to everyone in the office, in the family and in the friendship group, with no interest at all, it is easy to wonder whether it is worth going

---

1. C.S. Lewis *The Screwtape Letters* (London: Fount, 1998), p. 31-32.

on. Perhaps years and years of prayer have shown no obvious fruit. In the face of such frustration, knowing that the results were out of his hands kept Paul going. The job of the Christian speaker is simply to proclaim the Gospel.

The wide range of responses to the Gospel comes as a result of the devil blinding people. The person who thinks that science has disproved Christianity has been blinded by the devil. The person who thinks that Christianity has done nothing but harm to our culture in the last two thousand years has been blinded by the devil. The person who thinks that there is as much truth in Harry Potter as there is in the New Testament has similarly been blinded by the devil.

## 4. We are only slaves (v. 5b)

The *means* of Gospel ministry are considered here, and a close reading of this verse reveals a great surprise:

> with ourselves as your servants for Jesus' sake.

Whilst Christians might expect to be described as slaves of *Jesus*, here Paul declares to the Corinthians that he is *their* slave. The moment someone becomes *Jesus's* slave, they immediately become *your* slave. The reference here is to First Century slavery, not the horrific, brutal slavery of the Eighteenth Century. In the First Century, slavery was one of the chief means of employment and social security. Many First Century bankers were slaves (you might say not a lot has changed!), as were many medics. Since there was no system of state support, those who fell on hard times were sold, or they bonded themselves to somebody as their slave. Often people chose to go into this rather than to be employed on the open market. Paul says that when someone becomes a Christian, they are ultimately a slave to the Lord. And once they are a slave to Him, they are a slave to everybody else.

It would be incongruous to see ourselves in any other way. After all, consider how the Lord Jesus behaved when He came to earth. He *came not to be served but to serve, and to give his life as a ransom for many* (Mark 10:45). He washed His disciples' feet, something that only Gentile slaves did because it was so demeaning. And He said, *If I then, your Lord and Teacher, have washed your feet, you also ought to wash one another's feet. For I have given you an example, that you also should do just as I have done to you.* (John 13:14-15). Therefore, for someone who is following Jesus to boast proudly of being in charge of a group of people, and referring to the group as their slaves, is utterly inconsistent. And all the more so, when looking at the master whose hands were pierced, whose feet were nailed through, whose back was whipped, and who wore a crown of thorns.

The life of the Apostle Paul shows this principle in action. He had impeccable religious credentials: *circumcised on the eighth day, of the people of Israel, of the tribe of Benjamin, a Hebrew of Hebrews* (Phil. 3:5). His professional qualifications were matchless. He was a trained lawyer. His résumé guaranteed him a place at the top tables. But he worked with his hands as a tent-maker, so that he might not be a burden on those to whom he was proclaiming the Gospel.

This is the kind of authentic Christian ministry with which Paul wants the Corinthian church to align itself. Of course, there are many other forms of ministry posing as 'Christian' which might appear to be attractive alternatives. Our culture, like theirs, encourages us to place ourselves and our own needs at the centre of our priorities. We like to be served. But genuine Gospel ministry will involve being a slave to those we are serving. Paul wants the Corinthians, and us, to boast in the kind of Christian ministry that serves through the proclamation of the Gospel. It will not necessarily look that impressive on the surface – indeed, it will look 'slave-like', but it is the ministry that changes hearts.

## 5.  The impact is out of this world (v. 6)

Paul works out his slavery through proclamation. Verse 6 shows this ministry to be extraordinarily powerful. It should be noticed again that speaking ministry is explicit and up front here. Close examination of the verse shows that Paul is referring first to Creation. God brought light into being, from which life and every aspect of this global order derives its existence. He did not do that by reaching out a hand and switching on a light. Neither did He strike a match, nor take out a torch. He spoke. The God who spoke in the beginning and brought into being all of this creation, through our speaking of the Gospel message brings Regeneration, Justification, Illumination and Transformation. Ultimately He brings resurrection, and new creation. The ministry of Paul, as he makes himself a slave to those he serves in proclaiming the Gospel, is from God. It has an impact that is out of this world. God brings a whole new creation into being, for as Paul speaks the news of Jesus Christ, so God uses His words to create life-giving light in the heart of the non-Christian.

Sometimes people accuse those who seek to follow Paul in making the Word of God central to the ministry of their own life and that of their church as being 'one-tracked' or 'one-dimensional'. Surely, they say, there is more to Biblical ministry than a ministry of the Word? Paul would seem to suggest that there may be different aspects of an authentic ministry (all of which are initiated and inspired by the Word), but that an authentic Christian ministry will never be *less* than a ministry of the Word of God. It is the Word that gives life, it is the Word that sustains life, it is the Word that enables life, it is the Word that advances life. Why do evangelical Christians consider the Word to be so central? Because the Bible considers it so, God considers it so, and Jesus considers it so. How did God create life in the first place? He spoke! How did God meet Moses at the burning bush? He spoke! How did God redeem Israel? He spoke! How did God cause the dry bones of Ezekiel to come alive? He spoke! How did Jesus cause the lame man to walk (John 5), and Lazarus to come out of the tomb (John 11)? He spoke! Life, in the Bible, comes through the powerful Word of God.

One of the diagnostic tools that can be used to analyse any ministry is to ask: where do the leaders think the *power* lies?

Do they think that the power lies in the Word of God to produce genuine Christian experience, or that the power to produce Christian experience comes from somewhere other than the Word of God? If they think that the power to produce the experience lies outside of the Word, then all the energy of the week will be ploughed into producing an experience driven by some other means in the meeting on Sunday.

Do they think that the power lies in the Word of God to produce Christian community, or that essential Christian community is produced by some other means? If they think that the ultimate power lies in something other than the Word, then all the energy of the week will be committed to those other means, whether socials, relationships or shared interests.

Do they think that the power lies in the Word of God to produce Christian worship, or that real worship is enabled by some other means? If it is a confidence in other means, then all the energy of the week might be devoted to the songs, the musicians and trying to take people into God's presence on a Sunday morning.

However, if the leaders think that the power lies in the Word to produce authentic Christian experience, community and worship, then all the energy will be ploughed into the ministry of the Word. Substantial time will be devoted to prayer and preparation for a ministry that encompasses the pulpit, small groups and one-to-one work.

## Conclusion

The Corinthian letters identify many reasons for growing weary, losing heart, and throwing in the towel in Christian ministry: plans get frustrated; people are frustrating; proclamation seems so futile; opposition appears extremely fierce; our personal failings are obvious. It is into these sorts of situations that Paul speaks. He refuses to lose heart for: the ministry is God-given; the method is straight-talk; the results are out of our hands; we are only slaves; the impact is out of this world! Paul wants us to trust and boast in this kind of ministry. He doesn't want the Corinthians, or us, to lose heart and give up on the kind of ministry he's been describing. How tempting, when the going gets tough, to find a church or a ministry that is just a lot more comfortable, or that seems a lot more exciting, or less personally challenging. But Paul is adamant that we should stick with the real thing, for only the unchanged message delivered by the unchanging method of plain-speaking, servant-hearted explanation will have power to change the heart and work lasting change. Everything else is surface froth.

## Questions

1. What is it about the Gospel in verses 1 and 6 that causes Paul not to lose heart?
2. What are the two methods of ministry outlined in verse 2? What might these methods look like in practice today? Why might we be tempted to follow a ministry with *underhanded* methods?
3. How do verses 3 and 4 help us not *to lose heart?* What might be the consequences of not being clear on this?
4. How do verses 5 and 6 describe God's message and God's work? In whom does God work, and how does this grow our confidence in faithful ministry?

5. In the ministries of which you are a part, where do the leaders' energies suggest that they think the power lies? If you are leading a ministry, where does the commitment of your energy suggest you think the power lies?

# 4

# The Experience of Authentic Christian Ministry

## 2 Corinthians 4:7-16a

*⁷ But we have this treasure in jars of clay, to show that the surpassing power belongs to God and not to us. ⁸ We are afflicted in every way, but not crushed; perplexed, but not driven to despair; ⁹ persecuted, but not forsaken; struck down, but not destroyed; ¹⁰ always carrying in the body the death of Jesus, so that the life of Jesus may also be manifested in our bodies. ¹¹ For we who live are always being given over to death for Jesus' sake, so that the life of Jesus also may be manifested in our mortal flesh. ¹² So death is at work in us, but life in you.*

*¹³ Since we have the same spirit of faith according to what has been written, 'I believed, and so I spoke,' we also believe, and so we also speak, ¹⁴ knowing that he who raised the Lord Jesus will raise us also with Jesus and bring us with you into his presence. ¹⁵ For it is all for your sake, so that as grace extends to more and more people it may increase thanksgiving, to the glory of God. ¹⁶ᵃ So we do not lose heart.*

IN this section, Paul introduces us to his normal experience of Christian ministry. He does this with the intention that it commends him, both to the Corinthians, and to us. His is a ministry that looks and feels like death, with the surprise being that God deliberately chooses it to be this way. It is not by accident, nor is it an unfortunate turn of events, but rather it is by conscious design. Paul shows not only *what* authentic Gospel ministry looks like, but also *why* it looks this way. Image and appearance mattered hugely in Corinth, as they do today. Weak bodily presence was one of many criticisms that Paul's opponents levelled against him. It was no easier to have confidence in a death-like ministry then, than it is in the present day. Paul achieves his aim, that we do not lose heart with this type of ministry, by giving us three insights into it. Since the death-like experience is also that of every Christian believer, these verses additionally encourage us individually not to lose heart in light of our personal experience.

## 1. The Paradox of Christian Ministry (v. 7)

## Human Weakness: The Clay Pot

In likening himself to a *jar of clay,* Paul is not referring to the sort of expensive alabaster jar that might be found in a museum, nor the sort of feature plant pot that might be bought from the local garden centre. The 'jars of clay' referred to in verse 7 are almost certainly the clay pots in which candles were carried in First Century Corinth. The recent Pompeii exhibition at the British Museum included similar examples. They were exceedingly common and expendable items. They were highly fragile, easily chipped, and readily replaced. They cost next to nothing, and are the equivalent of today's disposable plastic cup.

## Divine Power: The Gospel

Paul has referred to the message of Jesus Christ as the light (4:4,6). It is the light of the truth of God which brings forgiveness and relationship with God. The crucified, risen and ascended Jesus Christ is the image of God: all truth is to be found in Him. The Gospel has the power to bring life rather than death (2:16), and it is more glorious than anything else in salvation history (3:7-11). The Gospel is therefore an enormously powerful and important light.

Verse 7 shows us where God has put the priceless treasure of the message of Jesus Christ: in Gospel servants. It is the combination of these two ideas that shows us the paradox of Christian ministry, which we might call 'Clay Pot' ministry. God places this glorious message in the equivalent of a disposable plastic cup. He wants us to know that anyone engaged in the work of Jesus Christ will always look and feel like one of these cups: weak, frail, fragile, and utterly normal. And yet, even as the Christian servant feels like that, the priceless treasure of the message of Jesus Christ will be shining out from them, just as light shone from the two-penny candle in First Century Corinth.

If this equation, where human weakness and divine power are held together, is not grasped, we will not be content with a ministry that visibly shows such human weakness. Publicly powerful and impressive ministries, with visibly striking leaders, will become more attractive. Such ministries could emanate from Lourdes, Rome, Toronto, or indeed anywhere that has not understood this paradox. It could even come from our own church.

If this pattern is not grasped in our own lives, we should not be surprised if we grow weary of authentic Christian service and genuine Christian living. Discontent and self-pity will flourish. When we experience hardship, as we inevitably will, we will think that we are getting the Christian life wrong, and we will move off to some other form of Christian message that looks triumphant and promises results without hardship. Even more seriously, we will teach a false gospel that gives other people a wrong expectation of Christian experience. Those who hear it will expect a Christianity that triumphs now, but will instead find they experience something different, where their weaknesses are unavoidable and unshakeable. Such disappointment undermines faith, and leads to losing heart.

## 2. The Experience of Christian Ministry (vv. 8 to 9)

Paul lines up four pairs of words in verses 8 and 9 to explain what 'Clay Pot' ministry feels like. In each case, the second word is far more powerful than the first, to demonstrate the mighty power of God. His point is obvious: Clay Pot ministry combines human weakness and divine power.

### *We are afflicted in every way but not crushed*

The Greek word translated here as 'afflicted' is a word used for the pressure of a large crowd pushing in, and infringing on personal space. It is used of the crowd in Mark's Gospel, pressing in on Jesus to such an extent that He has to get into a boat to teach (Mark 3:9).

In our family, we have a question that we sometimes ask each other: 'What size box are you in at the moment?' Not that anyone in our family spends their life in a box! Rather, how big is your space? How much pressure are you under? How pressed are you? If you are relaxed and easy, then you are in a big room. If life is moderately grim, you are in a cupboard. If things have reached breaking point, then you are in a matchbox. It is silly, but it makes the point.

Paul says that his normal Christian experience when engaged in genuine Christian work involves being afflicted. It is a matchbox experience. And yet, just as when the spiked ceiling moves closer and closer to Harrison Ford in *Indiana Jones and the Temple of Doom*, Paul finds himself *not crushed*. He experienced the power of God to deliver him, even though he was *afflicted in every way*.

### *Perplexed, but not driven to despair*

The second pairing in verse 8 starts with *perplexed*. The Greek word means 'uncertain'. Paul was at a loss, and unsure. It is used of the disciples in John 13 verse 22, when Jesus told them that one of their number was to betray Him, and they did not know whom He was speaking about. Such a feeling will be common to those who have faithfully served us. It is not a reason for us to distance ourselves from them. It is also not a hard word to understand for those who have themselves been involved in any sort of Christian work. It is the feeling of being at a loss, and being unsure how the ministry can go forward. The diary might be overloaded, preparation time might have disappeared, energy levels might have hit rock bottom, or resources might have dried up.

*But not driven to despair.* Not completely at a loss. In the midst of all the uncertainty, the mighty power of God sees that Gospel servants are *not driven to despair* as they proclaim the Gospel.

## Persecuted, but not forsaken

In the third pair of words at the start of verse 9, the word translated as 'persecuted' is a word that means 'to be chased after, pursued or hunted down'. This signals an increase in intensity. It is normal, not abnormal, for Christians engaged in God's work to find themselves under attack of some sort from people who want to silence them. This is something that has been seen increasingly around the world in the last 100 years, and has also been more observable on our own shores in this generation. In schools, there is significant pressure on Christian teachers to teach lessons that go against their beliefs and conscience. In many workplaces, approval is expected of diversity policies that do not accord with God's design, and the consequences of non-compliance can be severe. The current government is attempting to tackle 'extremism' through an adherence to 'British values'. Many Christians can readily identify the potential effects on the Christian's liberty, not only in the public square, but also in the home. However, in all of this the Christian is not abandoned by God, either in the present, or in eternity.

### *Struck down, but not destroyed*

*Struck down* translates a word from the boxing ring, or the field of combat. Knocked over, or struck down; but not perishing, or destroyed. Huge set-backs in the work might be experienced. Paul provides specific examples later in the letter that are examined subsequently in this book. In our own time and experience, the work at St Helen's suffered great set-backs in the 1990s when the building was struck twice by IRA bombs. What did it feel like to pick through the wreckage a second time? Paul's point here is that Clay Pot ministry will involve the church experiencing extraordinary set-backs. One commentator writes, 'Knocked down, but not knocked out.'

Before going any further, the words governing these four pairs should be noticed: 'in everything'. That is what the *in every way* means, and in the Greek, these words come at the start of verse 8. That is, it is not just in the most publicly visible aspects of his ministry of proclamation that Paul is hard-pressed, perplexed, persecuted and struck down. Rather, he experiences these things in every aspect of the work of making Jesus known in the world. This is the first of four such lists in the letter, which together makes this clear.

## 3. The Explanation of Christian Ministry: Living The Cross of Jesus (vv. 10 to 11)

Verses 10 and 11 contain significant parallels in respect of the death and the life of Jesus in relation to Paul's body. At first glance, verse 11 might appear to be a simple repetition of verse 10, but a careful reading shows the former to be in the active voice (carrying), and the latter in the passive (being given over). In verse 10, Paul actively takes up, literally *the dying of Jesus* in his body. Rather than being a one-off event, he is continually carrying the process of the death of Jesus. As Jesus set out for Jerusalem to suffer, be rejected and die, so Paul follows the same pattern. He is so convinced of the treasure of this message that he is prepared to take up the cross and give himself over to death, so that the life-giving message can be revealed as he speaks. In verse 11, Paul is given over to death. God is the implied agent, with this pattern of death not solely a matter of Paul's choosing. God laid the pattern of the cross on to his body. The same Greek verb, rendered in this verse *being given over*, is repeatedly used with reference to Jesus' relationship to the cross in Mark's Gospel. It is used both in the predictions of His death (Mark 9:31 and 10:33), and in the events themselves (Mark chapters 14 and 15), and is most frequently rendered *delivered*.

Paul is so clear that the truth of Jesus is essential to his hearers coming to know God, that he is prepared to be given over to extraordinary suffering by those who listen to him. He does this so that the message that brings light can be revealed as he speaks. In the letter, 'manifest' is used to refer to speaking about the truth of Jesus. So when Paul proclaims the Gospel of Jesus Christ, he is making an *open statement of the truth* (4:2). (The Greek root rendered *open statement* in 4:2 is rendered *manifested* in 4:11-12.) Similarly, in these verses, the life of Jesus is ultimately manifested through Paul's speaking, which he explains more fully in verses 12 to 15.

Paul is prepared to step out of his comfort zone, to be downwardly mobile, and to forego his rights, his reputation, and his rank. That has been his point all the way through this Corinthian correspondence. This pattern of death is right at the heart of his ministry. Paul proclaimed a crucified Messiah and his life was similarly cruciform. The challenge to the Corinthians then, and to us today, is to boast unashamedly in such a pattern of ministry.

It is enormously tempting for us to be hesitant in setting out this pattern before potential Christian workers. In interviews and conversations, we might rather try and impress them with their unique ability to do the job, and the satisfaction that they will get from it. But for Paul the issue is neither job satisfaction, nor personal comfort. The size, location, and smartness of the accommodation that he is to stay in are not of concern. Neither is the issue of personal fulfillment, nor whether his range of gifts might be widely used. He is not concerned with what he can get out of it, nor with how it might help his future ambitions. The issue is being a slave, wherever he finds himself, to whomever he proclaims the Gospel. In addition to asking us the question of whether we will support such a ministry, we are challenged as to whether we are prepared to be slaves to those we seek to reach. Will we live as a verse 10 and verse 11 person: actively taking up our cross, and passively ready to be 'given over' as we proclaim? Those preaching the message of the cross today can expect their pattern of life to be similar to Paul's.

Notice again the *always*. Just as verses 8 and 9 are governed by *in every way*, so verses 10 and 11 are dominated by *always*. It is easy to want to try and avoid such a pattern: perhaps by saving up enough money that could provide some insulation from tougher experiences; perhaps by looking to live in a particular sort of area, and not another; perhaps by trying to secure the children's entry into one particular school, and not another. Though we might try and bypass this stage of Christian ministry and life, we will find that we are not able to. As well as being the pattern for Paul and Gospel servants, this is the pattern of the Christian life for every Christian.

Having seen how tough this pattern is, the question must be answered as to why God makes it this hard. In a culture where image and appearance matter so much, why make Gospel proclamation look so weak and foolish?

Paul shows us three reasons, to convince us to not lose heart:

## a) Clay Pot Ministry shows the power belongs to God (v. 7)

The Greek word translated 'to show that' in verse 7 denotes a causal, purpose clause. God puts the treasure of the Gospel in jars of clay, so that it might be seen *that the surpassing power belongs to God*, and that the power of the message is nothing to do with us.

There are some forms of Christianity around today, that give the impression that God's way of operating is to remove from us all obstacles, all suffering, and all hardship. Publicity full of smiling Christians can sometimes give this impression. However, right through this letter, we find causal clauses, showing not only that God deliberately chooses to work through this Clay Pot model of ministry, but why. In chapter 1 verse 9 Paul says, *We felt that we had received the sentence of death. But that was to make us rely not on ourselves but on God who raises the dead.* In chapter 12 verse 9 Paul says, *Therefore I will boast all the more gladly of my weaknesses, so that the power of Christ may rest upon me.*

There is therefore no escape from this pattern. In the same way that the tributaries of a river are funnelled towards the estuary, and a prize plant is trained upward in one path, God boxes the Christian in, and insists that they experience Clay Pot ministry. God's church looks like a clay pot, and His people are self-evidently clay pots. This is all so that the power can be clearly seen to be from Him. Though attempts can be made to avoid the pattern, to duck it, and to move away from it, they are ultimately futile, because this is the pattern that God has ordained for Christian ministry. He entrusts His glorious treasure, the message of Jesus Christ, to ordinary, frail, weak men and women, so that the power of the Gospel can clearly and self-evidently be seen to be from Him.

Expectations should therefore not be for anything different to this pattern. This is God's economy. It is tempting to want to re-write the verses without mention of the *jars of clay*: 'We have this treasure. We are never pressed. We are never at a loss. We always know what we ought to be doing. We never find ourselves getting any hassle. We are never set back by anything.' Were it so, the whole process would be a simple, straight-forward progression from one glorious triumph to the next. But such a view is fatally wrong. If Paul had described a life like this, we would surely be marvelling at him. His work is currently read all over the world by billions of people, and his writing has been more influential in the lives of individuals than that of any other person in history. But Paul does not want us to look at him. He is at pains to tell us that he was just a clay pot, and that the power in his ministry was God's alone. We should expect faithful Christian servants today to be following a similar pattern. Furthermore, our suspicions should be aroused by any leader presenting a pattern of life and ministry that seems to be the opposite of this model.

How tempting it is to draw up a list of 'if-onlys', the achievement of which we imagine would result in the unhindered advance of the Gospel in our particular situation. It could be an improved online and social media presence, or a stronger political voice, leading to the election of a great Christian leader. The addition of a great Christian hero to the public square may be thought crucial to the unhindered advance of the truth of Jesus. At a more personal level, we might think that if only we could stop leading a particular house group, then our Christian ministry would be so much easier. It is tempting too to look back to some previous era and suppose, for instance, that in the Welsh Revival it was easy, or that in the early days of the First Century new churches just happened. It is tempting to think that if only I moved out of the city to a leafy suburb, then I could engage in God's work in a hassle-free environment.

However, Paul's point is that it is an essential part of God's econ-omy that human weakness and divine power are found together. The pattern is unavoidable. Paul tells us about himself to show us that this is normal. This is God's way of working, to demonstrate that the power is His alone. We should expect no sudden immunity.

## b) The life of Jesus is seen (vv. 10 to 11)

In each of the clay pot examples, there was relief and deliverance. In each case there was rescue from what might have been. Paul was not crushed, he was not driven to despair, he was not forsaken, and he was not destroyed. That rescue from those events, that deliverance, was *the life of Jesus.* God's deliverance now from despair and death foreshadows God's deliverance in the future, and the gift of eternal life.

This idea is exemplified in chapter 1 verse 9. Paul likens his experience of affliction in Asia to being dead. This caused him both to rely on God who raises the dead, and to look to God for future deliverance. Therefore, 'the life of Jesus' was displayed in him through God's deliverance. As Paul kept going in Gospel ministry, people would no doubt ask the question, 'How does he do this? He looks like he is never going to get back up. Where does he get the strength from?' Those who looked on, would see that it could only be the life-giving deliverance of Jesus. It would be easy to think that these sort of death-like circumstances are a disaster for Christian witness, without realising the significant life-giving impact they can have on others, when coupled with proclamation. Such deliverance should be understood as an encouragement not to lose heart. If Christians looked impressive in the world's eyes, it would be much harder to see the reality of Jesus' life-giving power.

The well-known nineteenth-century missionary Hudson Taylor had health that was described as delicate. Indeed, he went out to the mission field, but then needed to return because of ill health. Several of his children died as infants. Their mission premises were attacked, looted and burned with such vigour during one riot that the Royal Navy turned up to provide assistance. The dying of Jesus was hugely evident in the life of Hudson Taylor during his missionary endeavours in China. So too was the resurrection life of Jesus, keeping him going. Our challenge today is to boast and be confident in such servants who are similarly weak.

## c) The life of Jesus brings life to others (v. 12 to 15)

Verse 12 marks a notable shift. In verses 10 and 11, Paul has been saying 'death in us, life in us'. In himself, both the death and life of Jesus are displayed. In verse 12 he says again 'death in us', but in the second half of the verse he says, not life *in us*; but life is at work, *in you*. God works through Paul's sufferings, to bring eternal life to others. As Paul is afflicted, perplexed, persecuted and struck down – God is at work, bringing life to others. This life does not come automatically because of the sufferings, nor simply through Jesus' sustaining work in the midst of sufferings. The explanation of how life comes is in verses 13 to 15. It is a further unpacking of how the life of Jesus is manifested from verses 10 and 11. Life comes as Paul keeps speaking the Gospel!

Paul is convinced of the historical reality of the resurrection of Jesus, and knows that we will all have a future meeting with Jesus as Lord and Judge. This future meeting will happen, regardless of whether an individual chooses to believe that it will or not, and whether they like the idea or not. As a result, this knowledge and belief encourage Paul to go on speaking the Gospel, following the same pattern as the writer of Psalm 116, whom he quotes in verse 13 (*'I believed, and so I spoke'*). Like Paul, the Psalmist was in a death-like situation *the snares of death encompassed me; the pangs of Sheol laid hold on me* (Ps. 116:3). The Lord similarly delivered the Psalmist from his death-like situation *for you have delivered my soul from death* (Ps. 116:8). He believed that it was God who had delivered him from the predicament, and then spoke about the deliverance to others. The parallels to Paul's situation are clear, and they explain why Paul keeps speaking the Gospel!

While chapter 4 verse 13 shows similarities between what motivates Paul to speak out and the Psalmist, verse 14 identifies a further motivation behind Paul's speech, the fullness of which would have been unavailable to the Old Testament writer. The verse anticipates a day of future presentation, when believers will be raised with Jesus, and will be presented before God on the last day. It is a day also anticipated in chapter 11 verse 2, where the context of the only other use of this verb 'present' in 2 Corinthians is of a marriage day (the verb is rendered *bring* in the ESV in 4:14). The Corinthians will be presented, as a bride is presented to her husband, to Christ, by Paul. A day when *he who raised the Lord Jesus will raise us also with Jesus and bring us with you into his presence.* So Paul keeps speaking the Gospel!

Verse 15 shows us that this picture of the wedding day combines thanksgiving and glory to God. It will be a day of tremendous joy and celebration. Paul looks forward to this future wedding day, when the people of God who have trusted Jesus now, will meet Him as Judge and Groom. Therefore, every Christian man and woman has their own wedding day to look forward to. With the love, jealousy, commitment and protecting zeal of the bride's father, Paul will do anything to see that they remain pure, are not led astray, and are ready for this day. He takes up his cross, he is prepared to be given over to death, and he is ready to be hard-pressed, perplexed and struck down. He does not lose heart. He keeps speaking the Gospel!

## Conclusion

Clay Pot ministry combines human weakness and divine power. It is a pattern established by the Lord Jesus, and one that Paul has also demonstrably followed. Crucially, it is the form of ministry that has brought life to the Corinthian church. It was then of great concern that the Corinthians were in danger of being seduced away from this type of ministry.

Since believers today are similarly brought to life through ministries that follow this pattern, our priority must be to keep our confidence in what outwardly looks so weak. Now as then, the surpassing power being seen to be God's, the life of Jesus being made visible, and eternal life coming to others, provide the necessary assurance that God really is at work in the midst of such weakness.

## Questions

1. How do verses 7 to 12 follow on from Paul's description of the Gospel and Gospel ministry so far in the letter? What is the 'tone and feel' of these verses?

2. How do these verses encourage us not to lose heart in authentic Gospel ministry?

3. Read Psalm 116. How does Paul's use of it strengthen his argument?

4. Why do we struggle to associate with ministers and ministries that look like Clay Pots?

5. How does this passage shape our expectations about what the ministry of our local church will look and feel like?

# 5

# The Shape of Authentic Christian Ministry

## 2 Corinthians 11:16-12:10

*¹⁶I repeat, let no one think me foolish. But even if you do, accept me as a fool, so that I too may boast a little. ¹⁷What I am saying with this boastful confidence, I say not with the Lord's authority but as a fool. ¹⁸Since many boast according to the flesh, I too will boast. ¹⁹For you gladly bear with fools, being wise yourselves! ²⁰For you bear it if someone makes slaves of you, or devours you, or takes advantage of you, or puts on airs, or strikes you in the face. ²¹To my shame, I must say, we were too weak for that!*

*But whatever anyone else dares to boast of – I am speaking as a fool – I also dare to boast of that. ²²Are they Hebrews? So am I. Are they Israelites? So am I. Are they offspring of Abraham? So am I. ²³Are they servants of Christ? I am a better one – I am talking like a madman – with far greater labours, far more imprisonments, with countless beatings, and often near death. ²⁴Five times I received at the hands of the Jews the forty lashes less one. ²⁵Three times I was beaten with rods. Once I was stoned. Three times I was shipwrecked; a night and a day I was adrift at sea; ²⁶on frequent journeys, in danger from rivers, danger from* robbers, danger from my own people, danger from Gentiles, danger in the city, danger in the wilderness, danger at sea, danger from false brothers; [27] in toil and hardship, through many a sleepless night, in hunger and thirst, often without food, in cold and exposure. [28] And, apart from other things, there is the daily pressure on me of my anxiety for all the churches. [29] Who is weak, and I am not weak? Who is made to fall, and I am not indignant?

[30] If I must boast, I will boast of the things that show my weakness. [31] The God and Father of the Lord Jesus, he who is blessed forever, knows that I am not lying. [32] At Damascus, the governor under King Aretas was guarding the city of Damascus in order to seize me, [33] but I was let down in a basket through a window in the wall and escaped his hands.

12 [1] I must go on boasting. Though there is nothing to be gained by it, I will go on to visions and revelations of the Lord. [2] I know a man in Christ who fourteen years ago was caught up to the third heaven – whether in the body or out of the body I do not know, God knows. [3] And I know that this man was caught up into paradise – whether in the body or out of the body I do not know, God knows – [4] and he heard things that cannot be told, which man may not utter. [5] On behalf of this man I will boast, but on my own behalf I will not boast, except of my weaknesses – [6] though if I should wish to boast, I would not be a fool, for I would be speaking the truth. But I refrain from it, so that no one may think more of me than he sees in me or hears from me. [7] So to keep me from becoming conceited because of the surpassing greatness of the revelations, a thorn was given me in the flesh, a messenger of Satan to harass me, to keep me from becoming conceited. [8] Three times I pleaded with the Lord about this, that it should leave me. [9] But he said to me, 'My grace is sufficient for you, for my power is made perfect in weakness.' Therefore I will boast all the more gladly of my weaknesses, so that the power of Christ may rest upon me. [10] For the sake of Christ,

*then, I am content with weaknesses, insults, hardships, persecutions, and calamities. For when I am weak, then I am strong.*

THIS bonus chapter steps outside our core section (2:14 to 7:4), and is a deep study of chapter 4 verse 7 from both the Fool's Speech (11:16 to 12:10) and Paul's conclusion at the end of the letter. Chapter 4 verse 7 sets out one of the key principles of the letter: that God puts the treasure of the Gospel into weak Gospel servants, so that the power of the message can be seen to be His. In the previous chapter, we suggested that there are four passages that describe Paul's specific experiences of being a Clay Pot servant. Two of these are within the bounds of this core section (4:8-9 and 6:4-10), and set out the positive example of ministry. The other two are beyond this boundary (11:23-28 and 12:7-10), but nonetheless merit further consideration as they engage the false teachers more directly.

The subject of this chapter is something that fascinates all of us. It is valued, sought after and fought over: power. Every election is about power. Wars are fought over it. Billions of dollars are spent on power all around the world. Power is contested in every board room, classroom, hospital ward and lecture hall. But we are not looking at fleeting, passing human power. Rather, we are thinking about divine power, ultimate power and eternal power: God's power.

This chapter is called *The Shape of Authentic Christian Ministry*. It might also be called *the paradox* of divine power. It is an issue of real importance to us. Every Christian person wants to experience God's power, to be engaged in a ministry accompanied by God's power, and to go to a church that is enabled by God's power.

The point of this chapter is to show us that Gods' mighty power rests on, and is experienced and demonstrated in the context of abject human frailty and weakness. This is the economy of divine power! That statement can be pushed a little bit further. Paul argues that when God acts in supernatural power, He deliberately acts to make sure that those through whom He is at work, feel and appear weak, frail and inadequate. The aim then is that we will boast in, and be content with, the paradox of divine power.

This topic then brings us to the heart of the letter, the heart of the Fool's Speech, and the heart of chapter 4 verse 7. It is a lesson for the start of the Christian life, but it is so important, and so challenged by the world, that it is considered here.

## The Shape of Authentic Christian Ministry:

### 1. Deliberately Weak

The paradox is shown in chapter 12 verse 9a: *for my grace is sufficient for you, my power is made perfect in weakness*; again in verse 9b: *therefore I will boast all the more gladly in my weakness, so that the power of Christ may rest upon me*; and also in verse 10: *for when I am weak, then I am strong.*

This paradox is a repeated theme in 2 Corinthians, and there are 3 causal clauses in the letter that help us to grasp it:

### Chapter 1 verses 8 and 9:

*⁸ For we do not want you to be ignorant, brothers, of the affliction we experienced in Asia. For we were so utterly burdened beyond our strength that we despaired of life itself. ⁹ Indeed, we felt that we had received the sentence of death. **But that was to make us rely not on ourselves but on God** who raises the dead.* (Authors' emphasis.)

God deliberately brought Paul to the point of death, even as he was engaged in Gospel ministry, so that Paul should not rely on himself, but on God, whose mighty power was at work. God deliberately works to bring us to our knees, to make sure that the vessels through whom He works are consciously aware of their abject human weakness. God acts purposefully to keep His servants weak, so that the power might be seen to be His. Those who want to know the power of God will deliberately be made weak.

## Chapter 4 verse 7:

*⁷ But we have this treasure in jars of clay, **to show that the surpassing power belongs to God and not to us.*** (Authors' emphasis).

We have seen that the jar of clay was the First Century pottery item in which a lamp was carried around. The equivalent of the disposable plastic cup, they were weak, fragile and temporary. God has put the Gospel into these little crumpled plastic cups, to show that the surpassing power belongs to Him, and not to us.

This is a pattern that we see throughout the Scriptures, and not just in Paul. Gideon was the least important person in his father's house, and from the weakest clan of the tribe, yet was used by God to defeat His enemies (Judges chapters 6 to 9). Samson was born in a context of abject weakness, and was a man of obvious moral frailty, but who experienced the power of God (Judges chapters 13 to 16). King David was the youngest of Jesse's sons and a humble shepherd, yet he knew the mighty power of God (cf. 1 Samuel chapters 16 to 17). King Jesus *was crucified in weakness, but lives by the power of God* (2 Cor. 13:4).

## Chapter 12 verse 9:

*⁹ But he said to me, 'My grace is sufficient for you, for my power is made perfect in weakness.' Therefore I will boast all the more gladly of my weaknesses, **so that the power of Christ may rest upon me.*** (Authors' emphasis).

Before the causal clauses are considered any further, four vital qualifying statements concerning chapter 12 verse 7 should be noted:

*So to keep me from becoming conceited because of the surpassing greatness of the revelations, a thorn was given me in the flesh, a messenger of Satan to harass me, to keep me from becoming conceited.*

1. The Apostle Paul did not deliberately go out of his way to court weakness and suffering, in the manner of a religious martyr. It *was given* to him.

2. Weakness and suffering are not in and of themselves good. *A thorn was given.* Whilst God is sovereign, this thorn is *a messenger of Satan.* It cannot be said that God is evil.

3. Paul does not glory in the suffering, nor does he enter into some supernaturally induced trance-like state, where he seeks the suffering. Chapter 12 verse 8 makes that clear: *Three times I pleaded with the Lord about this, that it should leave me.* He does not glory in it, he does not court it, and it is not good in and of itself. Paul is here following a similar pattern to Christ in Gethsemane (Mark 14:33-36).

4. There is not an automatic connection between hardship, suffering and power, such that God is automatically working in divine power, simply because someone feels weak. Weakness does not guarantee that God is at work. Rather, God is in charge of all hardship and suffering. He deliberately acts to make sure that the human vessel through whom He works appears weak. In the whole of God's revelation, this is most powerfully seen at the cross.

The question to ask here is whether we really believe that this is the way God works; or whether we are Corinthian in our mind-set. In worldly Corinth, style not substance was the order of the day. The Corinthian celebrity culture glorified worldly wisdom and worldly power. Corinth took pride in powerful rhetoric. The Corinthian church was plagued by worldly Christian leaders, who are described as super-apostles (11:5), false apostles and deceitful workmen (11:13). But the worldly super-apostles boasted not in the Gospel of the crucified Christ, but in their own abilities and achievements. Today their boast might have been in the number of churches that they had planted, the number of people who attended their Sunday meetings, the size of their online following, or the sort of people who were part of their church. These types of claims are circulating in the church today, because we live in a worldly culture and we are surrounded by worldly ministry. Back then, style not substance was the order of the day in Corinth, because style not substance was the pattern to follow in Greek culture. Worldly qualifications, not Gospel clarity, were becoming the new norm and the key measure in church. People did not ask about the message that was taught, and whether it was the authoritative, delivered, once for all declaration of the ministry on the heart. They were asking the equivalent of whether the speaker looked good, whether he was funny, and whether he could fill the local arena. If the answers were yes, they concluded that he must be good. And some suspected Paul of walking according to the flesh (as he says in chapter 10 verse 2), because he appeared weak, and frequently had to change his travel plans, was often sick, sometimes felt insecure, and (perhaps his greatest drawback of all) was not considered a brilliant speaker.

Of those who preach on Sundays or give Christian talks in other settings, very few will be brilliant orators, or perhaps even 'natural' public speakers. But at whatever stage of ministry someone finds themselves, there is no sense in which that means Gospel servants should not keep working hard at their preparation and delivery. Paul is not advocating a resigned half-heartedness. Rather, the speaker will keep working both at clarifying and sharpening the content of their talk, and at delivering it in an engaging, accessible way for their particular audience. However, in so doing, they will be unlikely to match the rhetorical 'standards' of the day, and so might look or feel 'weak'.

A respected historian with a specialism in Fifth Century B.C. Greek culture has observed that there was a retro movement in First Century Corinth, harking back to the good old days of the great orators of a few hundred years before. The name of one of the most popular public speakers in Southern Greece in the First Century was Lucius Vibullius Hipparchus Tiberius Claudius Atticus Herodes. How impressive! We can almost hear him being introduced in the arena! Corinth was a worldly church, and we know from 1 Corinthians that they did not think that the cross was powerful or clever. The slide into the mindset that is being confronted in 2 Corinthians, of boasting in outward appearance and so wanting a worldly ministry, was almost inevitable. If the power in the message of the cross is not recognised, then it will be sought elsewhere, and something else will become the boast. Powerful orators and clever rhetoricians will be sought.

This then has a hugely contemporary feel. The more that is learnt of First Century Corinth from Paul's letter, the more closely its resemblance to Twenty First Century Western culture is seen. Image awareness, public relations departments, and marketing-driven mass-media are an established part of everyday life. Our arenas and stadia are filled night after night with such speakers. Modern political policy, with its light, substance-free philosophy, is marketed in a similar way. Our comedians, musicians, and sports stars are manufactured in the same way through carefully crafted public relations work. A worldly church, looking to emulate the world and impress its pagan audience, will act in the same way.

By contrast, Paul's ministry is clothed in weakness, sickness, failed travel plans and what are judged to be poor speaking skills. Cross-shaped as it is, Paul's ministry has become offensive to the Corinthian Christians. But, as God works in power, He deliberately locates His powerful Word in weak vessels. More than that, He deliberately acts to ensure that human vessels appear weak, so that the power and glory is unmistakably His.

I wonder whether we believe this and boast in this? I wonder whether we are content with this, and really believe that God's power is made perfect in weakness? Chapter 12 verse 9b sums up the whole of the Fool's Speech: *I will boast all the more gladly in my weaknesses, so that the power of Christ may rest upon me.* The *so that* shows that God's power will rest only as Paul recognises his weaknesses. It is a quite extraordinary power: the message has all of God's power to demolish strongholds (10:4). His message is one of eternal glory that brings life, and that promises the resurrection of our earthly tents that are wasting away day by day (4:16). His message looks forward to what is mortal being swallowed up by immortality (5:4).

Paul's opponents have made him out to be a fool. So in a way that is deeply ironic, and exceedingly clever, he goes out of his way here to boast in the way that a fool boasts, but with some proper Gospel boasting in verses 16 to 20. 'You've put me up to it. You've forced me to do it. If anyone's going to get a hearing, he must boast a little. Let me boast in the way that the sort of person you listen to boasts. It's a very worldly, fleshly thing to do. It's not the kind of thing that's written on the heart. It's the kind of thing that's on the surface. But let me boast, because everybody else is boasting. You bear with it when people take advantage of you. Come on, you foolish Corinthians, get real!'

## 2.  Unavoidably Weak (chapter 11 v. 21 to chapter 12 v. 4)

As Paul tells the Corinthians about his religious spiritual credentials in these verses, he boasts very differently to his boasting elsewhere. In chapter 11 verses 21 and 22, we are left in no doubt that Paul is a legitimate Jew, as he demonstrates that he has all of the religious connections that matter. Then in chapter 12 verses 1 to 6 he details his supernatural experiences. Boasting about visions, dreams or appearances of the Spirit gives leverage over others. Paul then speaks of his vision, in a bid to quell this misplaced boasting of some. He speaks as a fool, because only a fool would boast in this sort of thing. He would not normally tell them about his vision, but they have forced him into it. Any wise person would keep their vision to themselves. Paul would never normally speak to the congregation about it, because he would be in danger of appearing too fleshly. The supporters of Paul in the congregation can be imagined spurring Paul on, longing that he would describe in detail his substantial ministry résumé. But Paul simply cannot do that, because he is not a fool. The change of tone in his boasting in verses 23 to 33 reflects this.

Paul's boasting is utterly sarcastic. While knocking the legs from under the false teachers, it also raises the question of whether we would have gone to a church led by the Apostle Paul. There is no doubt that Paul taught the Gospel, but suffering, weakness, hard work, setbacks, human failure, not being a particularly gifted speaker, small numbers, the ordinariness of the church members, the failed church plants, the oppression from the world, and just the sheer hard work of it, might have made us hesitate. Remember that Paul did not court the hardship; he did not attempt to ensure that his planning was poor; he did not deliberately slack off in his communication so that his letters were dull and his talks were badly delivered. He sought to be all things to all people. In urban centre church work he sought to make what he did appealing to the sort of people he was trying to reach. But, the paradox of divine power is such that wherever God is at work in divine power, He will deliberately act to make sure that those involved in the ministry are weak, and that they feel weak, and that the ministry experiences weakness. There is a danger in our circles that we talk as if numbers have to be high, and speakers have to be funny and trendsetting. Impressive-looking pictures of our leaders and staff teams can be published, percentage success rates considered, and maps charted of our growing influence. How different Paul is in chapter 11 verse 30: *if I must boast, I will boast of the things that show my weakness.* This challenges us to consider how we think, speak, and talk of ministry.

As we have seen, we live in the modern equivalent of Corinth. There is no need to be an expert in First Century Greek culture to be able to understand Corinth. It is simply necessary to realise that since the Fall, human beings have always created fallen human culture. Corinth is just like London, and London is just like Babylon, and Babylon is just like the Plain of Shinar in Genesis 11, and the Plain of Shinar is just like Adam and Eve in the Garden of Eden. Wherever you find human beings in rebellion against God, you find fallen humanity and fallen culture. So because we live in a culture like Corinth and Babylon, there is a danger that we are not prepared to boast in the kind of ministry that Paul boasts in. It can be thought that the reason things have grown or developed, or Christians have become Christians, is because of our money, or our teaching programme, or our strategic thinking, or our leaders, or our leaders' oratory. A moment's thought shows the folly of this, because we know how weak we really are.

Across central London there are a number of lunchtime ministries proclaiming the Gospel, one of which started in 1997. One older Christian asked how the work was going, and was met with the response, 'I don't know how we're going to do it. I think it's going to kill us.' To which he just said, 'There's no Christian ministry without pain.'

This is a vital lesson for us. In every church family which I have known well, I can picture the congregation, family by family and individual by individual, and as I do so I am deeply conscious of our weakness both personally and corporately. There are always numerous examples of our human frailty and brokenness. One does not need to glory in these situations as if they were to be revelled in, nor does one need to seek out human suffering, or persuade oneself that they are in and of themselves good. But when God acts in power, He deliberately works to keep us weak. The cross provides the ultimate example of this.

This is weakness that the English trait of the 'stiff upper lip' finds difficult to acknowledge. There are many encouragements to us not to show weakness or emotion in the face of significant trials. Anecdotes of the end of the Battle of Waterloo, when Lord Uxbridge's leg was hit by a cannon ball, are held up as a pattern to follow. As the Duke of Wellington rode past, Uxbridge is famously said to have exclaimed, 'By God, Sir, I've lost my leg', to which Wellington replied, 'By God, Sir, so you have.' His stoicism and composure in the face of such loss and pain are seen as admirable, and all the more so when accounts of subsequent matter-of-fact surgical conversations are also retold.

The critique of this aspect of Englishness in no way encourages us to then portray ourselves as victims seeking pity, but it does allow a conscious awareness of sufferings. With a stiff upper lip, there can be no acknowledgement that we are weak; life is a journey from one triumph to the next. But actually, it is neither very Pauline, nor very Christian, to think that way. We do not need to assume a victim mentality, but we can admit that we are having a bit of a clay-pot week. *When I am weak, then I am strong. I will boast all the more gladly of my weaknesses.*

## 3. Persistently Content (vv. 6 to 10)

Paul writes about the great vision that he was given, and we have imagined his supporters longing that he would so boast in his true Spirit-filled ministry and experiences that his opponents would be silenced. But Paul will not do that. Rather, he says that he wants no-one to think too highly of him. He tells us about the thorn in the flesh that was given to him, and which made him so weak. The 'cross-light' Corinthians were forgetting the basics of how God works. The false teachers they were so keen on, with their high fees, had not suffered, and seemed so strong.

This raises the question of what we are content with. If we do not learn this foundational lesson of authentic Christian ministry, we will never stick with, or stick at, authentic and fruitful Gospel work. We will *lose heart* or grow weary. Verse 10 shows us that, as does verse 7, where Paul tells us that he was given *a thorn in the flesh*. There are a number of theories about what the thorn was: his eyes, his temperament, the heartache of false teachers, or some other physical disability. It is good that we do not know! It was given by God. Paul did not court it. It was altogether under God's sovereign control. It was a messenger of Satan. But God is not the author of evil. Martin Luther described Satan as 'God's dog on a leash'.

Among the most popular heresies of today is the idea that if you are suffering, there is something inadequate about your faith. Some of the most effective Christian leaders today suffer depression, or have permanent, deep sadness in their family, or struggle with their own apparent lack of interpersonal skills. If we begin to think, like the proponents of such views, that God's normal way of working is to operate to remove human weakness, a generation of Christians will be produced who think that God works in power through human strength. More than that, they will never be content. Countless ministers and ministries move on, because they have not learnt this lesson.

Paul's point here is therefore about contentment. He realises the weak and painful nature of ministry, and so he is not discontent. Chapter 12 verse 7 tells us that Paul sees this thorn as deliberately being given to him by God. There is a straight realism. Paul is not self-obsessed and always talking about himself. He is content. Unless we realise this key truth, that Gospel servants will always feel weak, we will always lack contentment, and we will want to move somewhere else. We will never be able to line up with and work in a lasting, effective, Christian ministry, because we will be looking over our shoulder. We might think that there would be a better place for us to go: perhaps to a different part of the city or to another region to live or work; perhaps a different type of work, or a more senior position; perhaps even a different country. Life would consistently be uprooted, and all because the lesson that a cross-proclaiming ministry will always feel weak, with hardship and perplexity the order of the day, has not been learnt. It is the pattern of the life of Jesus.

## Conclusion

This chapter has shown that when God works in power, He deliberately works to keep His servants weak. Such an understanding in His people will lead to a boasting in the right things, and contentment in present circumstances. There will be honesty, and a deep integrity about the ministry that is being done. The Gospel work will be persevered with, without discontentment, whinging, or looking over the shoulder. There will be prayerful dependence, recognising that there will be progress only if God works.

## Questions

1. How has this passage changed your expectations of what 'successful ministry' looks and feels like?
2. When someone asks you about the strengths of your church, what do you say? What are good things to 'boast' in? Where might we be tempted to 'boast' wrongly?

3. How does what Paul says about contentment change your attitude to the work you do, where you live, and what you expect for yourself and those closest to you?

4. Are there personal 'thorns' that you can identify in your own life? How does this passage help you to make sense of them?

# 6

# The Perspective of Authentic Christian Ministry

## 2 Corinthians 4:16–5:10

**4**[16] *So we do not lose heart. Though our outer self is wasting away, our inner self is being renewed day by day.* [17] *For this light momentary affliction is preparing for us an eternal weight of glory beyond all comparison,* [18] *as we look not to the things that are seen but to the things that are unseen. For the things that are seen are transient, but the things that are unseen are eternal.*

**5**[1] *For we know that if the tent that is our earthly home is destroyed, we have a building from God, a house not made with hands, eternal in the heavens.* [2] *For in this tent we groan, longing to put on our heavenly dwelling,* [3] *if indeed by putting it on we may not be found naked.* [4] *For while we are still in this tent, we groan, being burdened – not that we would be unclothed, but that we would be further clothed, so that what is mortal may be swallowed up by life.* [5] *He who has prepared us for this very thing is God, who has given us the Spirit as a guarantee.*

[6] *So we are always of good courage. We know that while we are at home in the body we are away from the Lord,* [7] *for we walk by faith, not by sight.* [8] *Yes, we are of good courage, and we would rather be away*

*from the body and at home with the Lord. ⁹ So whether we are at home or away, we make it our aim to please him. ¹⁰ For we must all appear before the judgment seat of Christ, so that each one may receive what is due for what he has done in the body, whether good or evil.*

IN 2009 the BBC ran an hour-long documentary on prospective Olympians for London 2012. Rower Katherine Grainger was one of the featured athletes. A particularly memorable scene was one shot before a February dawn. The ice was being scraped off the windows of her car before she drove to the training base, her breath visible on the air. As she sat at the wheel of her hatchback, shivering in her coat, the interviewer asked her, 'What on earth makes you do this?', to which she replied just two words: 'the podium'. The perspective of the podium shaped her life. She is now Katherine Grainger CBE (Commander of the British Empire), a six-times world champion, and shares the record as Great Britain's most decorated female Olympian.

Where we look as Christians will impact profoundly how we live as Christians. Proper Christian perspective results in pursuing genuine Christian service. In this passage, Paul wants us to have the perspective that he enjoys, which we have seen in chapter 4 verse 14: *knowing that he who raised the Lord Jesus will raise us also with Jesus and bring us with you into his presence.* For the Apostle Paul, Jesus' resurrection from the dead, in the past, guarantees our resurrection in the future. The finishing line governs his life, and it causes him to speak the Gospel, whatever the present cost, in spite of extraordinary opposition and hostility. Paul's courage to speak does not come from the fact that he is super-human. Rather it comes from this eternal perspective.

This perspective then enables Paul to *walk by faith, not by sight* (5:7), which is the key verse that unlocks this passage, and indeed much of the letter. The whole passage is constructed around the idea of walking by faith rather than by sight. In chapter 4 verse 18 Paul looks not to the seen but the unseen. In chapter 5 verse 1 he considers the longing for an eternal house, revealing in verse 2 that he yearns to be clothed with this heavenly dwelling. He shows a sense of homesickness for a future dwelling with God in verse 8. In verse 10 Paul shows the implications of future judgment for life today. Additionally, Paul's sphere of reference widens in this passage, from the previous focus on his own ministry, to believers in general.

Paul shows that this perspective of faith in the future, unseen reality, secured by the historical fact of Jesus' resurrection, produces in the Christian person three marks of authentic Christian experience. These are expressed by three fascinating pairs of concepts that are seemingly contradictory:

All of us will face **decay**, which Paul calls an outward wasting away (4:16). However, because we live by faith and not by sight, the Christian holds together with that experience of decay a daily **renewal** and perseverance.

All of us will face **death** (5:1), but because we live by faith and not by sight, we shall hold together with that experience of death an **intense longing** for our future home.

All of us will face the **homesickness** that comes from being distant from God in heaven (5:6), but because we live by faith and not by sight, we shall hold together with that homesickness an **accountability** before God.

These paired marks of authentic Christian experience further develop paradoxical ideas seen already (namely, that the great treasure of the Gospel is kept in weak jars of clay (4:7); and that the resurrection life and the suffering death of Jesus are being simultaneously experienced by Paul (4:10-11)). They are in direct contrast to the message of the false teachers, who took pride in impressive-looking visual, tangible, spiritual experiences. These contrasting pairs further explain why the sufferings of chapter 4 verses 7 to 12 are not a disaster. In those verses, the benefits of manifesting the life of Jesus are realised in the present. Chapter 4 verse 14 anticipates the future physical resurrection of the believer. The eternal implications of this, as expounded in chapter 4 verse 16 to chapter 5 verse 10, lead Paul to exhort us to be of good courage and not to lose heart. In the face of suffering, decay and death, there is both real hope and real purpose in Gospel ministry.

## 1. Renewal in the face of decay (vv. 16 to 18)

The perspective of the resurrection gives daily renewal in Christian service, in spite of every setback and hardship. Such future perspective leads to internal regeneration on a daily basis.

The word Paul uses for *wasting away* is a word used in Luke chapter 12 verse 33 to describe the destruction of a garment by a moth. Some people will be more acutely aware of outwardly wasting away than others, but Paul is not speaking here about simply growing old. Rather, he is speaking about troubles and wasting away as a result of serving Jesus. In chapter 4 verses 7 to 15, it was seen that the normal Christian experience of serving God will be an experience of hardship and difficulty: hard-pressed, perplexed, persecuted and knocked down.

Paul is therefore no escapist dreamer. He realises and preaches that Christian ministry is hard work. But, as these troubles are faced with the perspective of faith, it can be seen that being battered and bruised as a result of serving Jesus, is part and parcel of being on the road to eternal glory. These hardships do not earn Christians a place in heaven, but are a necessary part of belonging to Him. Our Christian life is therefore not deficient when we suffer, nor have we deviated from God's best path for us. Rather, such suffering is the normal experience of the Christian life, while we wait for glory.

While an awareness of being battered and bruised may not be the case for everyone at a particular point in time, some will be very conscious of troubles of one sort or another in Christian service. This might be a particular recognition of outward wasting away, frailty, and inability in serving Jesus. Paul does not make light of such troubles, but he does realise that these pains are causing him to fix his eyes on what is unseen. And as he does so, the perspective of faith causes him to realise that the troubles, in comparison to the weight of glory, are light and momentary (v. 17). Using measures of time and weight, the glory that is being prepared is shown to be incomparably superior. This is in no way to minimise the pain and hardship of the suffering. It is, however, to provide a right perspective on them. Despite frequent setbacks, there is a certainty and security never enjoyed by those pursuing a sporting podium.

Without such a future perspective, we will give up in the Christian life. This is also not to suggest that we must simply grin and bear it, and just walk around glumly as we wait for the resurrection. Considering the resurrection brings refreshment, renewal, revival and restoration.

This is the heart of authentic Christian renewal. Sometimes the term 'renewal' is used to refer to a particular style of worship, or to a particular use of gifts within the church. However, this section has shown the work of renewal to be connected to the inner transformation brought by the Spirit, and the life-giving deliverance of Jesus. True renewal is about seeing the present in the light of the future, and so persevering. It is about being renewed day, by day, by day. The remedy when we are tempted to give up is not withdrawal from serving Jesus. Rather, verse 18 tells us that it is to look to the things that are eternal and unseen.

## 2. Intense longing in the face of death (vv. 1 to 5)

The present experience of groaning in the face of death is unmissable in these verses. In verse 2 and verse 4 Paul is speaking about the reality of our own mortality. In verse 1 he speaks of his body as an earthly tent, and he is contemplating the destruction of his body. In verse 3 he speaks about being found naked, a common way at the time of referring to the death and destruction of the body. In verse 4 he openly speaks about what is mortal.

However, since Paul lives by faith, governed by an eternal horizon, he knows that God has an eternal, physical body for him in heaven. There is no dualism. His earthly, short-term tent is going to be transformed into an eternal, long-term house. Therefore he groans, longing for this exchange to take place. He wants a resurrection body, rather than the separation of his body and soul.

Verse 1 makes this point vividly: the temporary dwelling of a flimsy tent is exchanged for a permanent residence. The longing for a substantial dwelling place is a common experience. It may come while lying under the canvas, with the rain still thundering on the roof mid-way through week two of the holiday. The ample time for reflection has clarified the folly of agreeing to indulge your husband's boyhood dream of taking the family camping in Wales. Such longing may also be experienced while persisting in a rented flat, and wishfully gazing at the online profiles of properties that are completely out of reach. However, for the Christian, the permanent residence that is longed for is not a house made of bricks and mortar, but a resurrection body.

Paul expects this sense of longing for a future, solid reality to persist in the life of all genuine Christians, as they contemplate their own death and mortality. The longing has two aspects to it: groaning in expectation, mixed with groaning in the agony of being weighed down by the present reality of death and mortality.

Once again, Paul's realism is striking. This is no escapist dream. Paul is only too aware of his own mortality. Daily, hourly, he faces the reality of his frail, earthly body. But in the face of his mortality, the normal, authentic Christian experience is one of groaning, of dissatisfaction, and of longing for the future.

Notice how contrary this is to the false teachers in Corinth, who lived in the opposite way. They operated by sight and not by faith, boasting in visible, outward appearances, and not in the work of the Holy Spirit in believers' hearts. But Paul tells us that the authentic work of the Spirit is to cause us to groan in expectation, and to groan in agony, whilst we grow increasingly dissatisfied with the limitations of our present mortal state. There cannot be any one of us who is not aware of our own mortality. The recent growth in the fitness, beauty and health industries is evidence of the intense dissatisfaction of this current age with its physical state. The work of God's Spirit in Christians only multiplies the dissatisfaction. The normal Christian experience is of groaning while longing to be clothed, of becoming increasingly discontent, and of becoming increasingly future-focused.

## 3. Accountability in the face of homesickness (vv. 6 to 10)

If verses 1 to 5 concentrate on the necessary faith required of Christians in relation to their bodies, verses 6 to 10 focus in on the faith required with respect to the Christian's relationship with God. The picture in verse 8 is one of homesickness. The Christian man or woman will have a profound sense of not being at home in this life, and so will be longing for heaven. Christians have a sure and certain relationship with God, even though He cannot be seen today. Therefore, Christians must live by faith, yearning for the day they will be able to see the Lord and have a perfect relationship with Him.

The temporary separation of human relationships can provide a small picture of this. If a husband and wife are briefly apart, perhaps for reasons of family or work, there will be a longing to be together again. While modern communications allow significant contact to be maintained, physical proximity is what really counts. The homesickness of children can also follow a similar pattern, whether on a first overnight trip away from home, a first term at university, or the first night in a new home. Human relationships can show significant parallels in absent homesickness, but reunions will never achieve the perfect relationship for which everyone longs. Only a face to face relationship with the Lord can deliver this perfection.

However, rather than leading to hopelessness and simply biding the time, verses 9 and 10 tell us that the believer seeks to please the Lord whilst they are still in their earthly home. Verse 10 provides the reason for wanting to please the Lord: the appearing before Christ's judgment seat, a meeting that every believer will experience. The reference here is to the family judgment that believers will face on the last day. This, along with the practical outworking of this accountability, is the subject of the next chapter.

Regularly today, people are sceptical and cynical about the idea of living by faith as described by Paul, suggesting that Christians are simply playing a game of 'let's pretend'. Such accusers seem to imagine that during the week Christians live life on one plane, a rational one, and at the weekend they remove all their rational faculties and enter into a fantasy world. Lewis Carroll managed to capture this popular misunderstanding of faith in his book, *Through the Looking Glass*. The White Queen asks Alice to believe that she is 'just one hundred and one, five months and a day'. When Alice protests at being asked to believe something so ridiculous, the Queen replies: 'Try again: draw a long breath and shut your eyes'. Alice is not persuaded; 'One *can't* believe impossible things,' she says. To which the Queen replies:

'I dare say you haven't had much practice…When I was your age, I always did it for half an hour a day. Why, sometimes I've believed as many as six impossible things before breakfast.'[1]

In encouraging the Christian to keep living by faith and not by sight, Paul is not foreshadowing the White Queen in asking us to believe six impossible things before breakfast. Rather, living by faith means to walk on the basis of what God has revealed to be true. Though often described as taking a leap into the dark, it should be rightly understood as stepping into the light. It is God's revelation that has caused Paul to *know* (4:14 and 5:1) and to have *good courage* (5:6,8). Here, in particular, it is what God has revealed about the resurrection and the Holy Spirit.

We have already seen that chapter 4 verse 14 gives the historical fact of the physical resurrection of Jesus as the grounds for confidence that in the future the Christian will also be physically raised with Jesus. It is on the basis of Jesus' resurrection that eternal glory (4:17), a resurrection body (5:1) and a future day of judgment (5:10) are guaranteed.

The present reality of the Holy Spirit in the life of Paul and of the Corinthians also fuels Paul's faith. They have been given the Holy Spirit as a guarantee that God will keep His promises (1:22), particularly around being given resurrection bodies (5:5). The Holy Spirit has also enabled them to understand the death of Jesus and to want to live for God. He has given them a longing for the future, and has transformed the Corinthians into a publicly attestable letter of recommendation, *to be known and read by all* (3:2).

Today much of the teaching about the Spirit is focused on the present feelings and the present sight of the individual. Assessment

---

1. Lewis Carroll, *Alice's Adventures in Wonderland & Through the Looking-Glass*, Collector's Library, 2004.

of someone's spiritual condition is made on the basis of how they feel, and what they see, in the present. One recent study of the prosperity gospel cites E.W. Kenyon as teaching that 'Christians could look to the cross not as a promise of things to come, but as a guarantee of benefits *already* granted.'[2] To those who follow in the wake of Kenyon such as Joel Osteen, T.D. Jakes, Creflo Dollar and Joyce Meyer, the mark of God's Spirit at work is to be found in the present health, wealth and happiness of the believer. However, Paul tells us that the Spirit's work will cause Christians to live by faith and not by sight. The renewal that the Spirit brings will be for ongoing Christian service in the face of extraordinary opposition. He brings a longing for future glory, while groaning in the present. It has been rightly said of the 'Prosperity Gospel' that its main problem is one of timing. It brings God's promises for future blessing into the present. Paul's Gospel is radically different – as was Christ's example (cf. 13:4).

These two things then, certainty about the resurrection and the presence of the Spirit, enable Paul to say: *We know; we are always of good courage; we walk by faith and not by sight.* Sometimes people say, 'I wish I had your faith'; or 'If only I could believe, like you'. Paul's point is that the perspective of faith comes from knowing and being convinced of the resurrection of Jesus, and from the confidence that this knowledge and conviction have come from God's Spirit at work in the life of the believer.

## Conclusion

Walking by faith and not by sight is the key idea of this section. Despite the compelling evidence for such a manner of life, many today dismiss such belief as fanciful. Such a heavenly perspective produces in Christians three marks of authentic experience: an

---

2. Kate Bowler, *Blessed*, OUP, 2013, p. 17.

outward wasting surpassed by an inner daily renewal; an intense longing for an eternal, physical body when confronted with their own death and mortality; and while feeling a profound sense of not being at home, there is a right sense of accountability before God. The contrast between Paul and the outwardly impressive false teachers on this matter is stark; the latter might be described as living by sight. As we consider ministries that we encounter today, this concern for and confidence in a ministry centred on the unseen, eternal reality provides a valuable benchmark.

## Questions

1. In what ways does Paul's concern for the unseen, eternal realities help us to see what sort of ministry we should put our confidence in today? What sort of ministry should this encourage us to avoid?

2. How might this perspective on the present and the future shape our prayers for Gospel servants today?

3. How does our culture try to defy ageing and death? How does Paul describe the Christians' bodily experience? How is this hope better than one focused purely in this world?

4. How do these verses help the Christian to be of good courage while they wait to be with the Lord? In what sort of circumstances might this encouragement be particularly precious?

5. How does this passage reinvigorate our desire to live to please the Lord?

# 7

# The Scope of Authentic Christian Ministry

## 2 Corinthians 5:6–6:2

**5** *⁶ So we are always of good courage. We know that while we are at home in the body we are away from the Lord, ⁷ for we walk by faith, not by sight. ⁸ Yes, we are of good courage, and we would rather be away from the body and at home with the Lord. ⁹ So whether we are at home or away, we make it our aim to please him. ¹⁰ For we must all appear before the judgment seat of Christ, so that each one may receive what is due for what he has done in the body, whether good or evil.*

*¹¹ Therefore, knowing the fear of the Lord, we persuade others. But what we are is known to God, and I hope it is known also to your conscience. ¹² We are not commending ourselves to you again but giving you cause to boast about us, so that you may be able to answer those who boast about outward appearance and not about what is in the heart. ¹³ For if we are beside ourselves, it is for God; if we are in our right mind, it is for you. ¹⁴ For the love of Christ controls us, because we have concluded this: that one has died for all, therefore all have died; ¹⁵ and he died for all, that those who live might no longer live for themselves but for him who for their sake died and was raised.*

*[16] From now on, therefore, we regard no one according to the flesh. Even though we once regarded Christ according to the flesh, we regard him thus no longer. [17] Therefore, if anyone is in Christ, he is a new creation. The old has passed away; behold, the new has come. [18] All this is from God, who through Christ reconciled us to himself and gave us the ministry of reconciliation; [19] that is, in Christ God was reconciling the world to himself, not counting their trespasses against them, and entrusting to us the message of reconciliation. [20] Therefore, we are ambassadors for Christ, God making his appeal through us. We implore you on behalf of Christ, be reconciled to God. [21] For our sake he made him to be sin who knew no sin, so that in him we might become the righteousness of God.*

**6** *[1] Working together with him, then, we appeal to you not to receive the grace of God in vain. [2] For he says,*

> *'In a favourable time I listened to you,*
> *and in a day of salvation I have helped you.'*

*Behold, now is the favourable time; behold, now is the day of salvation.*

THROUGHOUT this study of 2 Corinthians we have suggested that Paul's aim in writing is to keep the Corinthians lined up with his ministry. This section shows that aim most clearly, as chapter 5 verse 12 holds what we consider to be the key verse of the book. It is as if Paul is holding up a plumb-line to the Corinthians' ideas about Gospel ministry. This picture comes from the building trade, where a plumb-line is used to test whether walls are being built straight. When it is your own building work under scrutiny, the plumb-line can be a daunting instrument, as it tells you whether you are building the Leaning Tower of Pisa, or something that is straight. Here Paul is performing that test on the Corinthians' understanding of ministry. It is as if Paul is also holding up a plumb-line to our understanding of the Christian faith and Christian ministry, asking whether we are in line with true Biblical ministry.

2 Corinthians chapter 5 contains four particularly famous verses:

Verse 11  *knowing the fear of the Lord, we persuade others*

Verse 14  *the love of Christ controls us*

Verse 17  *if anyone is in Christ, he is a new creation*

Verse 21  *he made him to be sin who knew no sin, so that in him*
*we might become the righteousness of God*

Each of these verses would justify a chapter to itself, but our purpose here is to see the force of these verses together. Paul is directing the verses towards the Corinthians as he speaks about himself, because he wants them to boast in the kind of ministry that is driving him, as he is controlled, driven forward and incentivised by the love of Christ. Therefore, it is not just to the leading lights in a group that he is speaking. He wants the whole church to line up behind this heralding Gospel ministry.

## 1. The Coming of Christ (vv. 6 to 13)

The coming of Christ controls the form of Paul's ministry. It brings accountability before God for how he spends his time. Paul's point here is that Jesus is Lord. He has been crowned Lord and Judge of all. He has defeated death, ascended, been crowned King, and He will return. Therefore, one day, every single one of us will meet Jesus face to face. *We must all appear before the judgment seat of Christ* (v. 10). And because Paul is so convinced of this clear future appointment, for everybody, before the Lord of all, he engages in plain-speaking proclamation: *we persuade others* (v. 11). In these verses there is both a sense of accountability for Paul himself (vv. 6 to 9), and also a sense of the accountability of Paul towards everyone he meets.

The termly practice of reading school reports is a little like this. The child brings the report home and presents it to their parents, who then take time to consider it. The achievements in the report never affect whether or not the child is still a part of the family. But different degrees of diligence and success in working, in light of their given abilities, will be recognised. Such parental interest and recognition is ultimately a loving thing.

However, Paul is also conscious that we must *all* appear before the judgment seat of Christ (v. 10). The Father has entrusted to the Son the business of judgment, so that each one of us may receive what is due for what he has done in the body, whether good or evil. So those who have rejected Christ will meet Christ as their judge. That will not be a friendly, family homecoming. That will be the most terrifying, cripplingly stomach-churning, anguish-ridden, fearful encounter with the living God, for those who have rejected their Lord and King.

Jonathan Aitken, the former Conservative minister convicted of perjury, talks about the day that he met the judge, and did not get away with it. Those convicted go down into 'the cage' under the Old Bailey, so called because it is just a barred cell. Everyone who has been convicted that day is there. When Aitken got to the cage, there was a grown man, sitting in the corner, with his head in his hands, weeping. Another man was holding the bars of the cage, banging his head against them. Anguish. Fear. Judgment. Horror. Therefore driving Paul, and driving all true Christian ministry, will be this sense of personal homecoming, of accountability and judgment. Paul cannot look out on the world without seeing the spiritual reality of the Lordship of Christ, and there is therefore an urgency that we persuade others.

Notice how this impacts the nature of his ministry. In verse 11 Paul says that, *Knowing the fear of the Lord, we persuade others*; and *if we are beside ourselves*, if we are out of our minds, *it is for God* (v. 13). In other words, if a person does have some sort of extraordinary spiritual experience, and is 'beside themselves', it is given to them for their relationship with God. It is *for God*. This stands in contrast to how Paul conducts himself when he is with the Corinthians. Paul would never dream of using such an experience to promote his ministry. In his relationships with people, he seeks to persuade, and is self-controlled. Any kind of hyper-spiritual experience is very much in private, between himself and God. Paul would never use this gift publicly, because he wants to persuade people. It is the verbal declaration of this public announcement that persuades people that they are going to meet God in judgment, and that they need to be reconciled to Him today. Such persuasion is also an authenticating mark of a Gospel servant. Descriptions or demonstrations of supernatural experiences neither legitimate a ministry, nor proclaim the message of salvation that all people need to hear.

Paul is then very, very careful about the way that he deploys his spiritual experiences. Pagan Corinthian society was very impressed by oratorical skills. Spiritual Corinthian society thought that experiences of the mind were something really special. But Paul says that they are not something that he is going to demonstrate publicly or mention. Rather he is simply going to speak plainly, publicly declaring the truth, because he knows that he is going to meet God, and He is going to ask him how he got on. 'You had fifty, sixty, seventy years. How was it? How did you use it?' Similarly, all believers know that they, along with the people to whom they speak, will meet God. All believers will similarly be asked about how they got on, and so should have a similar ambition, wanting to explain the Gospel clearly and simply. Showing off supernatural gifts should not feature in this context.

There is accountability in many types of work, perhaps an annual appraisal, where the worker is summoned before the boss, to review how they have got on. Many will bumble along for ten months of the year, and then will become a frenetic, frantic hive of activity in the last two, in order to try and impress the person to whom they are accountable. But when we come before the Lord and Judge of all, there is a sense of year-round accountability. He will be interested in how we perform in every minute of every day. Paul says in his mind, all the time, 'I'm going to meet Him, His truth is written on my heart, and I seek to persuade.'

Our technology bombards us with continual reminders, notifications and updates. There is a sense in which the Gospel should be a continual reminder to us, at all points of the day. Whether as the alarm goes off in the morning, or over the breakfast table, or passing a neighbour in the street, or when travelling to our destination, or where we spend most of our day – at every point, we should remember that *we must all appear before the judgment seat of Christ* (v. 10).

The point is not that everybody has the responsibility to be a pulpit preacher, but Paul does want all Christians to line up with his ministry. If that were done, everyone would see themselves as a full-time Christian worker, with a responsibility to line up their energies, prayers, imagination, gifts, financial resources, time and diaries, to make Jesus Christ known as Lord of all.

## 2. The Cross of Christ (vv. 14 to 16)

In these verses we discover how the cross of Christ impacts the shape and scope of Paul's ministry. He serves anybody, anywhere, at any cost, because Jesus died on behalf of all.

'Controls' in verse 14 is in the King James translation 'constraineth'. It translates a Greek word which means literally 'to push together, and to drive forwards'. When a toothpaste tube is squeezed out, there is only one way the toothpaste can go, because it is constrained. Similarly, when a river approaches a gorge, there is only one way that it can go, because it is constrained. The love of Christ, the death of Jesus on the cross, constrains Paul in much the same way.

In the second part of verse 14, Paul writes: *because we have concluded this*. Paul knows of the crucifixion of Christ, and he has meditated on it, he has thought about it, he has prayed it through, he has pondered it and he has really chewed it over. So this lifestyle of Paul's is not something that just happened and fell on him out of the blue, mystically. He has thought about the death of Jesus, and has drawn conclusions. It is what he sees in the death of Jesus that drives his ministry. So if someone says, as people frequently do, 'I'm slightly weary, I've lost heart', or 'I'm feeling very dry. I'm going through a difficult period, I haven't got the zeal I used to have', here is the answer, at least in part. Meditate on, think about, chew over, and be convinced of what happened at the cross.

What is understood from verses 14 and 15 must bring the reader to the same conclusion that Paul reached in verse 16. Everywhere we go, everyone we look at, wherever we are, we see in a particular way because of what we conclude from the death of Jesus. Our view of *everyone* is affected, not just a small group here or there.

The love of Christ controls us, so there is a new governing feature in the whole of our life. No longer should family, career, reputation or pleasure control us as Christians, because we have concluded that one man, Jesus, has died, literally 'on behalf of everybody'.

These are not easy verses: at first glance they may look as though they are teaching universalism, that the death of Jesus means that everyone will be saved. That cannot be the case, and the parallelism helps us to see why:

| verse 14 | ... *one has died for all* ... | ... *(the) all have died* |
| verse 15 | ... *he died for all* ... | ... *those who live* ... |

The *all have died* of verse 14 are then described as *those who live* in verse 15, something that is only true of Christians. Additionally, there is differentiation between the groups in both halves of the parallel.

In the first half of the parallels, when Paul says *one died for all* and *he died for all*, it is clear that *all* refers to all people everywhere. *God so loved the world, that he gave his only Son* (John 3 v. 16). *He is the propitiation for our sins, and not for ours only but also for the sins of the whole world* (1 John 2 v. 2). As Paul Barnett says, 'through the death and resurrection of the "one," Christ, the deathly effects to "all" of the sin of the "one," Adam, are overturned, at least potentially.'[1] In the second half of the parallels, Paul includes 'the' in front of both groups, literally '*the* all have died' and '*the* living ones,' which the English translations do not pick up. This must refer to a particular group who have actually responded to the truth that Jesus died on behalf of everybody.

This then means that the Shape and Scope of ministry should be considered in light of the cross.

## The Shape of ministry

Those who are spiritually alive realise what the cross means, and therefore cannot go on living for themselves. The cross moulds and shapes everything about the way they see the world. Paul gets up in the morning and remembers that he is accountable to God, and that Christ died as an atoning sacrifice on behalf of the sins of the whole world. There is one God; there is one mediator between God and man who gave His life as a ransom on behalf of all. The consequence is that Paul cannot look at anybody in the same way again.

Christians have died to living for themselves. It is a constant battle, but as they meditate on the cross, they are slaves, constrained by the love of Christ. Paul had a résumé for which to die, but he chose to die for Christ. He went to Corinth, but not as a top barrister; as a tent-maker, he was doing the equivalent of shelf-stacking, so that he could proclaim the Gospel. Putting your career first is a

---

1. Barnett, *2 Corinthians*, p. 290.

fundamentally pagan idea. The idea that anybody who has died to self should speak about 'my career' as their defining ambition is profoundly un-Christian. The thing that controls the world is often this self-absorbed obsession with 'my career'. However, the thing that should control the Christian who understands the cross of Christ is not 'where am I on the career ladder? How much am I earning? How did I do in the end of year review?' Rather, it should be the love of Christ that controls and constrains, such that a Christian cannot look at anybody in the same way again. The people a Christian sees in their place of work, or at the school gate, or on their street, are all going to meet God in judgment; and Christ died on behalf of them.

## The Scope of ministry

The *all* of verse 14, which is universal, drives the *no one* of verse 16, which is also universal. Paul wants us to line up with this cross-shaped, selfless, sacrificial ministry, so that we realize that Christ died for people in every nation, whether South Africa, Namibia, Botswana, Lithuania, Latvia, Estonia, China or Japan. Christ died for people in every condition, whether divorced, single, married or remarried. Abused or abuser. Christ died for every generation, whether parent, grandparent, child or teenager. Christ died for every profession, whether plumber, teacher, office worker, nurse or shopkeeper. He died for all, and so we must go to all. This may be a perspective that has been lost. If it has been, the answer is right here in these verses: *because we have concluded this*. I have thought about the cross, so this is how I understand the world.

R.A. Torrey was an outstanding personal worker, who wrote a book on how to work for Christ.[2] His approach to personal work merits being quoted here at length:

---

2. R.A. Torrey *How to work for Christ: a compendium of effective methods* London: James Nisbet & Co (1901).

'Where to do it: in the homes, on the streets, in the parks and other resorts, on a walk or a ride, at the place of business, on cars and boats … Travelling on the steam cars affords a very rare opportunity for personal work. Travellers usually have much time which hangs heavily upon their hands and are glad to get into conversation with anyone. But if one is a real Christian, there is one subject always uppermost in his mind. One subject which he would rather talk about than any other, and that is Jesus Christ. When you get into a train, get as good a seat for yourself as you can, put your coat and grip out of the way, move over to the far side of the seat, and make the vacant space beside you look as inviting as possible. If the car is at all crowded you will soon have a fellow passenger, and the desired opportunity for personal work. Sometimes it is well to keep your coat or grip in the seat beside you until you see the man or woman that you want coming and then remove them and move along in the way of silent invitation. It is as well to talk with the trainmen and porters. They are usually willing to talk.'

Such a mind-set and ambition is a huge challenge to us today. Torrey cannot have been English, or a Londoner!

## 3.  The Commission of Christ (chapter 5 v. 18 to chapter 6 v. 2)

Of all the parts of the letter, this short section is the most densely packed. In it, Paul lays out the very heart and essence of his understanding of Christian ministry and the Christian life. It is a purple passage! Here it is seen that the Commission of Christ controls the appeal that Paul makes. It is here that Paul shows us the heart of the Gospel.

It can be seen straight away from verses 18 to 19 that Paul's ministry is concerned with reconciliation. The idea of reconciliation is something that everyone is familiar with, in all walks of life. When two people have a disagreement in the office, when a husband and wife have a disagreement at home, when two players fall out on the pitch, reconciliation and a restored relationship are sought. The relationship spoken of in this passage is not a human relationship between men and women, but a relationship between God the Creator and us, the created. The heart of genuine Christian ministry is the reconciliation of this relationship.

## The urgent need for reconciliation with God: a relationship in ruins

The language that Paul uses in verse 19 assumes that apart from Jesus Christ, our relationship with God our Creator lies in ruins. *In Christ God was reconciling the world to himself, not counting their trespasses against them.* Without the work of Jesus, God counts our trespasses against us. The word translated as 'to count against' speaks of God's right, just, measured judgment of our rejection of Him. It is not a fit of pique; it is not a human rage. It speaks of a settled, steady judgment against all that is wrong. 'Count against' in the Greek is a term from the financial world, and speaks of a mounting debt that has grown up which demands repayment. Lawyers and accountants who charge by the minute have clients with bills counting against them. Students see their loans increasing book by book, film by film and pint by pint. The Greek term translated as 'trespass' means primarily 'a false step'. It is a blunder or a deviation, a wandering from uprightness and truth. It is a relational word when used in the Bible, concerning our deliberate and wilful doing of the things that God hates and not doing of the things that God loves.

Outside of Christ, our trespasses count against us, and there is a debt outstanding. That has to be the case, because if someone has done the things that God hates, and not done the things that God loves, then their relationship with Him lies in ruins. That would be true of any relationship, but with God, things are far, far more serious, because He is our Creator. He is just and pure; He has to judge all that is wrong, and He cannot just sweep our transgressions under the carpet. It follows that if someone fails to treat Him and those He loves in the way He loves, it has huge implications for them the creature, and for their relationship with God.

God says of Jesus His Son, *This is my beloved Son; listen to him* (Mark 9:7). It follows that if someone refuses to listen to God's Son Jesus, and blocks their ears to Him; and if they refuse to do the things Jesus loves and do the things that Jesus hates, then their relationship with Him is in ruins. Jesus says of Himself, *Whoever does not honour the Son does not honour the Father who sent him* (John 5:23). So if someone persistently, consistently and wilfully refuses to honour the Son, the relationship has been wrecked. Paul is not talking about a human being whose standard of justice is relative and can fluctuate. Rather he is talking about the pure, perfect and spotless God, who judges justly, and who will not and cannot sweep our failures under the carpet. Apart from Christ, our trespasses count against us.

This idea of the need for reconciliation is sometimes illustrated through the positioning of two chairs. To start with, the chairs are facing each other. God is described as sitting in one chair, and the individual in question in the other. A perfect relationship is represented. However, sin means that we have turned away from God, and are facing in the opposite direction, with the back of our chair facing God. Reconciliation is then sometimes described as a matter of the individual simply turning back to God. However, a close study of verse 19 shows that cannot quite be right, for the verse suggests that there is a double turning of the chairs. The individual has turned away from God and their trespasses are evidently there. But God also counts their trespasses against them, and He is therefore angry in judgment against them. It is as if God has also turned His chair around. Therefore, any reconciliation must deal with both of these turnings, and is not solely a case of the individual needing to turn back round.

## The perfect means of reconciliation – the relationship restored

The whole point of Paul's work according to this passage is to hold out the offer of a restored relationship, in and through Jesus Christ. It is God who has done this work of reconciliation. God is the initiator of reconciliation, Jesus is the agent who has secured reconciliation for us, and we are the beneficiaries.

Verse 21 explains how it is that God achieves this reconciliation. God made Jesus Christ on the cross to be treated as if He were us. Jesus Christ never did anything that God hates. He always did everything that God loves, and He knew no sin. But for our sake, God the Father made God the Son to be sin, which meant He had to be punished for our sin, so that in Him, we might become *the righteousness of God* (v. 21). Our trespasses, that were due to count against us, were counted to Jesus, so that God could look on us in Christ, and declare, 'You are perfect. I count you as righteous.'

The key words in verse 21 are *for our sake.* They speak of a swap, a substitution and a great exchange, as Christ, the sinless one, carried our sin to the cross, and was punished for it. It is as if God has a diary of our lives, and within it are recorded all the actions that have flowed from our attitude towards Him and Jesus Christ. All the deeds we have done. All the things we should have done, but have failed to do. And the things we have done that He hates. It makes awful reading. But as I look at the diary, and as I turn to the front cover, instead of finding 'William Taylor' written on the front cover, I find the words 'Jesus Christ'. There is then another diary, with all the beautiful, wonderful deeds that Jesus Christ Himself did. The perfect life, the loving thoughts, the wonderful actions. As I turn to the front cover, instead of finding 'Jesus Christ' in the front of it, I find 'William Taylor'.

The idea of an individual benefitting from the actions of another, by joining themselves to that person by faith, can at times be difficult to understand. However, all of us are used to benefiting from the actions of other people. Think back to the London Olympics. 'We've won twenty-nine gold medals.' 'We've just won the 10,000m.' Almost all of us made absolutely no contribution to the effort, but because we are from Great Britain, the athletes were doing something on our behalf, which we then benefited from. Our benefiting from somebody else's action is not an alien idea. As someone turns to trust in Jesus Christ, they find that on the cross, God has made Him to be sin for them. Jesus carried God's judgment on all of my trespasses on His shoulders on the cross. As I trust in Him, and allow Him to carry the weight of my trespasses, so God counts me as righteous.

It is important to be clear that this is not a legal fiction. Some have complained about this concept of counting someone as righteous, and have suggested that God's forgiving of our sin through Jesus dying on the cross is as if God has a spell of divine amnesia, forgetting about our sin and sweeping it under the carpet. But God does not forget about our sin. On the cross, Jesus carried our sin and was punished for it. Neither is this conferring of status a legal fudge. Again, people have complained that God is pouring out His judgment on an innocent third party. If a person had done something unspeakably wrong against you, and you then brought judgment on someone else, then that would be a legal fudge. But God is not pouring out His anger on an innocent third party. Jesus Christ was fully human and so in the death of Jesus, God was punishing a representative of humanity. Christ Jesus was wholly divine and so, in the death of Christ, God was carrying the judgement owed to Him in His own being. Furthermore, Christ and the believer are spiritually united together. This has come about by faith, and the Christian is then indwelt by the Spirit of Christ. At the cross, God the Father fully satisfies His own judgment, by pouring out His judgment on God the Son, in our place.

A young man from another country had a near perfect marriage with a woman he loved deeply. Their friends described them as a perfect couple. She trusted him, he loved her. One night, on a one-off trip to London with a team of colleagues, he did something that he will regret for the rest of his life. He went to a church the next day, and when talking about it, he was at a loss to find words to describe the stupidity of it. It involved an office outing, a great deal of alcohol and another woman. He was unable to get the words out for the tears of shame. He longed for reconciliation. But of course, if there was going to be real and genuine reconciliation, then his wife would have to find some way to deal with the anger, the hurt, the damage and the sheer repulsion. She was rightly, justly angry, and some way needed to be found for reconciliation to take place.

Verse 21 tells us that God has found a way for reconciliation to take place, and that it is a just way of restoring our relationship. At the cross, He who knew no sin, became sin for us. It is a loving, pure and perfect way of restoring our relationship. God has taken the initiative, Christ is His agent, and we can be the beneficiaries. The person who has just come to understand the cross clearly for themselves for the first time, can now say, 'Jesus died for me', and put their name into this verse. There is great encouragement in doing this, whether as the newest Christian or the most mature believer coming to the end of their earthly life. To paraphrase chapter 5 verse 21: 'For my sake, God made Jesus to be sin who knew no sin, so that in Jesus I might become the righteousness of God.'

## A right time for reconciliation – now!

To the question of when we should be reconciled to God, Paul says, 'Now! Today!' If you are not in a reconciled relationship with God, through Jesus Christ, today is the day to seize the moment, to turn to Christ, and to put your trust in Him.

Things could be left here, but this passage contains one of the most shocking wake-up calls in the New Testament, which some of us may need to hear. Up to now, this idea of Paul's ministry of reconciliation has not been tied back into its context in this letter. When Paul first went to Corinth, he would have made a Gospel appeal to them along the lines we have just read. He would have said to them, 'Now is the moment of reconciliation. God has made it possible through Jesus Christ. You can have a restored relationship. Trust Jesus.'

Reading chapter 5 verse 20 to chapter 6 verse 2 again, we need to answer the question, 'to whom is Paul writing?'

It seems extraordinary, but Paul is appealing to the Corinthian church! That is where the challenge of this passage lies. Paul is not saying that all Christians are ambassadors, though that may be true in a secondary way. Paul is saying that God has made him, the great Apostle, an ambassador, holding out to the world the offer of reconciliation with God. Then he turns to the Corinthian church and says, 'I am making the appeal to you, Corinthians.' But they are already Christians. Surely they are already reconciled to God! The key lies back in chapter 5 verse 12, where it was seen that the Corinthian church were ceasing to boast in the Apostle Paul and his message of the resurrection and the death of Jesus Christ. Instead they were drifting into boasting in another kind of Christian ministry that was really glamorous and looked exciting, but which was no longer teaching Jesus Christ crucified and risen. Therefore Paul turns to them, and says, 'if you are drifting from me, and if you no longer boast in my message, if that is no longer your delight and joy, it is as if you need to be reconciled to God all over again.'

This sort of drifting might be seen in various ways today. Perhaps someone used to go to a church that taught the Bible clearly week by week. They once believed firmly in the cross and resurrection of Jesus Christ, and once took the ministry of Paul seriously, and sought to listen to Paul and what he has to teach us. But as they took to their study of academic theology, for some unknowable reason, they began to distance themselves from Paul, no longer treating Paul's writing as Scripture, and openly disparaging Paul and putting him down, saying things like, 'Oh yes, I used to be like you, but I've moved on.' The study of this passage reveals the appropriate response: *we implore you on behalf of Christ, be reconciled to God…we appeal to you not to receive the grace of God in vain…Behold, now is the favourable time; behold, now is the day of salvation* (5:20–6:2).

Perhaps someone describes themselves as a Christian, but when it comes to the shape and form and substance of their Christianity, they consider Paul to be 'a bit extreme, a touch over-zealous, rather dogmatic and slightly exclusive. Not the kind of Christianity I would want for my children. He's not very British.' Again, this sort of person needs to be reconciled to God.

For the Corinthians it may well be that their most recent encounter with Paul both through his visit and then via the 'severe letter' which called for repentance, meant that they were drawn to alternative styles of ministry and that they distanced themselves from Paul. That being the case, Paul says to the Corinthians: 'be reconciled to God'! And Paul is clear that such a reconciliation will come about only as they are reconciled to him and his ministry. That *be reconciled* is passive, shows that this reconciliation is ultimately the work of God. He is the one who does not count trespasses against us (5:19), on the basis that Christ became sin for our sake (5:21). The call is therefore to receive this reconciliation, and then to continue in it. As in any church today, this call is made both to those who seem to have embraced this reconciliation, that they would persevere in it; and to those who might not have received it so far.

## Conclusion

Paul's expectation is that every individual, church and Christian organisation will be proactively, imaginatively and energetically committed to the advance of the Gospel, through the proclamation of the Gospel, for the honour and glory of Jesus.

It is the future appointment of all Christians before Christ's judgment seat, and the ensuing accountability, that spurs Paul on to make Jesus Christ known as Lord of all. Paul has meditated on the cross of Christ, and it is this realisation of what the cross means, that Jesus has died for all, that shapes how Paul views people. His concern is whether someone is reconciled to God, and the scope of his ministry sees him taking the Gospel to all.

So this letter, to a Christian church, comes as something of a wake-up call to us. As we hold up the plumb-line, do we still live with a right heavenly homesickness, longing to be in heaven with Christ? Do we see ourselves now as no longer living for self but living for Christ? Do we see ourselves as a new creation, made by Jesus Christ to serve Him and to work for Him? Paul says that if we find ourselves drifting from Paul and his Gospel message of reconciliation, then we need to take care that we have not received God's grace in vain.

*For our sake he made him to be sin who knew no sin, so that in him we might become the righteousness of God.*

## Questions

1. This passage contains one of the strongest wake-up calls in the New Testament. To what extent do you think that you personally need to hear it?

2. How conscious are you of the accountability that you have towards God? How does Paul model living in light of this?

3. Spend some time meditating on the cross, praying that God will grow your convictions about the conclusions that Paul makes here.

4. What can hold you back from wholeheartedly playing your part in persuading people to be reconciled to God? How do the motivations of this passage encourage you?

# 8

# The Allegiance of Authentic Christian Ministry

## 2 Corinthians 6:3–7:4

**6** *³ We put no obstacle in anyone's way, so that no fault may be found with our ministry, ⁴ but as servants of God we commend ourselves in every way: by great endurance, in afflictions, hardships, calamities, ⁵ beatings, imprisonments, riots, labours, sleepless nights, hunger; ⁶ by purity, knowledge, patience, kindness, the Holy Spirit, genuine love; ⁷ by truthful speech, and the power of God; with the weapons of righteousness for the right hand and for the left; ⁸ through honour and dishonour, through slander and praise. We are treated as impostors, and yet are true; ⁹ as unknown, and yet well known; as dying, and behold, we live; as punished, and yet not killed; ¹⁰ as sorrowful, yet always rejoicing; as poor, yet making many rich; as having nothing, yet possessing everything.*

*¹¹ We have spoken freely to you, Corinthians; our heart is wide open. ¹² You are not restricted by us, but you are restricted in your own affections. ¹³ In return (I speak as to children) widen your hearts also.*

*¹⁴ Do not be unequally yoked with unbelievers. For what partnership has righteousness with lawlessness? Or what fellowship has light with darkness?* <sup>15</sup>*What accord has Christ with Belial? Or what portion does a believer share with an unbeliever?* <sup>16</sup>*What agreement has the temple of God with idols? For we are the temple of the living God; as God said,*

*'I will make my dwelling among them and walk among them,*
 *and I will be their God,*
 *and they shall be my people.*
<sup>17</sup>*Therefore go out from their midst,*
 *and be separate from them, says the Lord,*
 *and touch no unclean thing;*
 *then I will welcome you,*
<sup>18</sup>*and I will be a father to you,*
 *and you shall be sons and daughters to me,*
*says the Lord Almighty.'*

**7** <sup>1</sup>*Since we have these promises, beloved, let us cleanse ourselves from every defilement of body and spirit, bringing holiness to completion in the fear of God.* <sup>2</sup>*Make room in your hearts for us. We have wronged no one, we have corrupted no one, we have taken advantage of no one.*

<sup>3</sup>*I do not say this to condemn you, for I said before that you are in our hearts, to die together and to live together.* <sup>4</sup>*I am acting with great boldness toward you; I have great pride in you; I am filled with comfort. In all our affliction, I am overflowing with joy.*

THE subject of this chapter is our allegiances and alliances in Christian service and living. Here, the questions are answered of whom we should line up with in our work for Jesus, and whether everyone who calls themselves a Christian should always be united with everyone else who calls themselves a Christian.

This passage is one of the most heartfelt and passionate appeals of the New Testament. It is an appeal from the Apostle Paul, to the Corinthian church he founded, to line up with authentic Christian ministry and with the way in which he serves the Lord Jesus: *In return (I speak as to children) widen your hearts also* and *Make room in your hearts for us.* Simultaneously, Paul commands them to cast off and depart from other allegiances: *Do not be unequally yoked with unbelievers* and *Therefore go out from their midst.*

This issue is far more significant than simply a matter of church politics. In chapters 3 to 5 of the letter, Paul has laid out authentic Christianity. He has made his appeal as an ambassador appointed by Jesus Christ, and he has urged this church to be reconciled to God. Paul has God-given teaching that enables a person to be reconciled to their Creator. He speaks a message about the death and resurrection of Jesus such that the person who accepts His Gospel has access to eternal life.

The image of the envoy, or the ambassador, is an excellent one for making the point. An ambassador speaks with the voice and the authority of the one whom he represents. This is demonstrated on our television screens whenever there is an unfolding diplomatic crisis, or if a war seems imminent, because it is so often the ambassadors of the countries involved who are interviewed. The automatic assumption of those watching is that ambassadors speak on behalf of the country they represent.

Therefore, this is not simply a matter of church politics, or tribes, or preferences, or minor likes and dislikes. The stakes are substantially higher, and the consequences are of a far greater weight. Looking back to chapter 5 verse 20 reminds us of this: *We implore you on behalf of Christ, be reconciled to God.* Paul implores this church, which he founded, and which now wants to distance itself from him, to be reconciled to God. It might have been thought that they were already reconciled! This serves as a reminder that if anyone distances themselves from Paul and his teaching, they need to be re-reconciled to God, because they are distancing themselves from the authentic Gospel.

They need to come back to the heart of the Christian faith that Paul outlined in chapter 5 verse 21: *For our sake he made him to be sin who knew no sin, so that in him we might become the righteousness of God.*

The particular context into which Paul was writing should be remembered. There were factors both pushing and pulling the Corinthians into false ministry. Since first preaching the Gospel in Corinth, Paul had subsequently made a *painful visit* (2:1). He had written a 'severe letter' (2:4) and it seemed that there had been some genuine repentance (7:6-9). Nonetheless he remains nervous about his third visit (13:1) for fear that genuine repentance may still be needed. So, then, Paul with his message of repentance was not easy to be around! It is not comfortable to listen and respond to a message demanding real change. It is easier to cling on to lives and lifestyles lived in opposition to God, rather than align them with the authentic Gospel. In this turbulent situation there were preachers who claimed to be Christian, but preached a different Jesus, a different Spirit, and a different gospel. Theirs was a ministry that seemed to demand less of its hearers, but Paul describes them as servants of Satan (11:15).

This has particular and profound application for us, as we operate in this phase of Christian history in the West. The mainline denominations of Western Christianity are going through a period of major moral and doctrinal upheaval, particularly around the sphere of sexual ethics. For example, there are powerful forces within the Church of England who are eager that the denomination bends to the will of the secular state, and changes its views on human sexuality, gender roles and marriage. Where these forces encounter those like the Apostle Paul, who are adamant that the Christian Gospel requires and demands real and radical repentance and obedience to the faith, those who are seeking such change are urging those who disagree to 'walk together' and to find means of 'good disagreement'. They are advocating that a Christianised form of the sexual ethics of the world be embraced. It is precisely this language that we must 'walk together' and that we must find 'good disagreement' that is in absolute conflict with what the apostle Paul says here. *Do not be unequally yoked with unbelievers* (6:14); *Therefore go out from their midst* (6:17). These imperatives are not advocating 'good disagreement'.

Paul's appeal, then, is that we check our assessment of him the Apostle, and that we then change our allegiance.

## 1. Check your assessment – his credentials are authentic (chapter 6 vv. 3 to 10)

Paul begins with this appeal to check our assessment of himself and of his ministry. Verses 3 to 10 contain a long list describing different aspects of Paul's experience. He has already shown us his doctrinal teaching. Now he shows us the standard of ministry that he has adopted. His point is that there is no difference between the message he preaches and the ministry he practises. He is asking us to check our assessment of him, such that having laid out his doctrine in chapters three to five, we will now find that there is no distance between this doctrine and the way that he conducts his ministry. The form of Paul's ministry is entirely framed and governed by the message he preaches.

There are four key groups of factors, each an inevitable consequence of believing in and being engaged in the God-given ministry of reconciliation that Paul has outlined in chapter 5 verse 21. Together they demonstrate that Paul is 'the real McCoy'.

## Pain and Persecution for the sake of the Gospel (vv. 4 and 5)

Suffering and hardship might seem like a strange place for Paul to start. However, because Paul has an urgent message from God to proclaim to people everywhere, and because that message is radically challenging to our world, inevitably his ministry will be marked out by hardship and suffering.

Chapter 5 verse 21 has expounded the message that God graciously, kindly, mercifully, has given His Son Jesus to pay the penalty for our rebellion against Him. This is so that we might be put into a right relationship with Him. It has been called 'the great exchange', as it speaks of Jesus Christ bearing the penalty for our rebellion, and of our being given the purity and righteousness of Christ in exchange. It is glorious good news for everybody, for there is no way that anyone could ever earn their way to heaven. The authentic Christian church, therefore, should expect to follow the pattern of both Paul and Jesus, and will always be ready to stop at no personal cost in order to make this message known. The authenticating marks of Paul's ministry are hard work, suffering and sleepless nights. It stands to reason, for if someone has a message that is glorious news for the whole world, they will stop at absolutely nothing to communicate it.

But whilst the message is glorious good news for those who will accept it, it is a radically challenging message. The world hates this message of genuine Christianity. Verse 21 tells us that everyone is a rebel against God, that everyone deserves to face God's anger for their rebellion, and that God has appointed one specific person and nobody else to deal with this great problem of rebellion. That message is not popular. People do not like to admit that they need God's help. They hate to acknowledge that they have a need. They do not want to say that they have gone wrong. And so, inevitably, authentic Christian work involves the hardship and trouble of verses 4 and 5. Just as Jesus suffered at the hands of a hostile world, so the Christian messenger will suffer.

Sometimes towards the middle of a year in ministry, people who are engaged in Christian work for the first time experience something of a crisis: 'It's such hard work! There seem to be such great sacrifices! I have to stay up late, and give up certain social activities. My career sometimes looks like it might suffer.' That is exactly so. When Christians have such a message of good news which the world hates, it will be normal for Christian ministry to experience trouble, hardship, stress, beatings, imprisonment and riots.

The lesson that hardship and suffering are authenticating credentials of Christian ministry may have to be learnt again and again. Notice how Paul introduces his list – *by great endurance*. It is therefore not what someone *once* did, as a student or as a teenager, but what they do now. Do they boast in these credentials? Is this what they want for their children? Will they prioritise a ministry that puts Jesus first, over career, qualifications, and university places?

## Authentic Spirituality (vv. 6 and 7)

It does not come as a surprise that one of the authenticating criteria of Christian ministry is the power of God and the Holy Spirit. Indeed, it would be surprising if they were not characteristics of authentic Christian ministry! But what is surprising, is what Paul chooses to put alongside the power of God as characterising the work of the Spirit and the work of God. At first glance, it all seems to be rather un-dramatic: *by purity, knowledge, patience, kindness,…. genuine love, by truthful speech.* But for Paul, evidence of the Holy Spirit and the power of God are authenticated in his life by the qualities listed here. Authentic Christian ministry flows out of an authentic Christian message, and results in authentically Christ-like actions.

There was a time recently when a denomination was making demands for powerful, physical healings in church, as if they are the authenticating mark of the Holy Spirit's work. Such requirements misunderstand the work of the Spirit; they are not what authenticate a ministry. This passage links back to chapter 5 verse 21 again, because the ministry of the Holy Spirit is the ministry of righteousness, as the study of chapter 3 demonstrated. The Spirit brings to us this great message of the possibility of a relationship with God; He enables us to accept it, and He produces righteous actions within us. There is nothing undramatic about producing pure minds, pure words, pure actions, pure motives and pure imaginations. This change is authenticated by kind acts, kind thoughts and kind words, and is marked out by sincere love. There is nothing weak about producing truth in word and deed. And Paul says, 'you've seen that in me'. *We commend ourselves in every way* (v. 4). Paul does not see music, atmosphere or dramatic events as authenticating credentials of Christian ministry, but rather *purity, knowledge, patience, kindness* – actions produced by the powerful work of God as His Spirit brings the message of chapter 5 verse 21.

## Persistent Proclamation (vv. 7 and 8a)

Paul here describes his clear and plain-speaking proclamation as one of his *weapons of righteousness.* The *truthful speech* of verse 7 shows us that proclamation is to be understood within these *weapons.* Here, as in chapter 10, Paul does not have in mind physical weapons of warfare. Rather, he likens speaking the Word of the Gospel to being armed with a sword and a shield. Paul persists and perseveres with proclamation despite extraordinary opposition. In every situation, no matter what the prevailing circumstances, whether people speak well or ill, whether times are good or bad, whether Paul is received with gratitude or ingratitude, he continues to speak this message about Jesus. Sometimes they herald him as an ambassador of God, and receive him with great glory and honour. Sometimes people send the most horrendous reports back home about Paul. But he will not put a spin on his message to ensure a better reception. He will not change the message to suit his listeners. He simply seeks to persuade people through plain proclamation.

*The Times* columnist Matthew Parris unfavorably describes a type of politician who will change their message to appeal to what they think people want to hear: 'I simply cannot stomach the sight of people who call themselves leaders, sniffing around the pollsters and focus groupies, in a craven attempt to ingratiate themselves with what they reckon to be the opinions of the mob.'

Paul will not do that! He does not mind how popular he is, or what his reception is. He will simply proclaim the message of Jesus Christ. Clearly. Persuasively. Simply. With substance, not spin. He is an ambassador who comes with a message which he does not change. That is what ambassadors are to do: stay 'on message'. They will not shift to suit whoever they are speaking with. They are not at liberty to change that message. The credentials that prove that they are authentic have nothing to do with the novelty or excitement, adaptability or flexibility of changing the message to fit with the country to which they go. This is very important for our age. As the reception of the Christian message becomes more and more hostile in our current Western World, here is the test of the authenticity of the messenger. Will they change the message, or put a spin on the message, or loosen the message, in order to make it more acceptable? Will they dress it up? Will they depart from the work of prayer and preaching? Or will they simply, with the weapons of prayer and persuasive proclamation, get on with the work of the Gospel regardless of the reception?

## Gospel Perspective (vv. 8b to 10)

Seven pairs of apparently incompatible opposites are listed in verses 8b to 10. The point with each of these pairs is that through the spectacles of chapter 5 verse 21, Paul's apparent position of absolute failure and defeat is to be seen as a position of great victory. And therefore Paul rejoices, he lives on and he keeps going in spite of all appearances to the contrary.

Paul is regarded as an imposter in verse 8, but he is genuine, because he is teaching the message. He is regarded as unknown to God, yet because of the Gospel message that Jesus has died for our sins, he knows that he is known to God. He is regarded as dying, yet because of the message of Jesus Christ, he lives on. He is beaten, yet he is not killed. He is regarded as sorrowful, and he might easily be down in the mouth. Yet because he has got his 'Gospel glasses' on, he is full of joy, because he has realised that suffering is part of speaking the truth about Jesus. He is regarded as poor because he has turned aside from the career prospects and the glitter that the world has to offer. Yet he knows that he is immeasurably rich, as he engages in the casual workforce, and proclaims Jesus Christ.

Here then is Paul's analysis of his authentic Christian ministry. He has presented us with the credentials that commend the authentic Christian worker. It is important to notice the differences between how Paul judged the value of the ministry going on in a church, and the measures of our age, which the writings of one contemporary broadsheet columnist disclose: the architecture; the sermon; the music; the spiritual high; the liturgy; the after-service care. There are indeed some categories of common concern: the place of the sermon and the message that it proclaims were evidently crucial to Paul. The music and liturgy also allow substantial scope for Gospel-centred encouragement and building up. However, whether a Christian ministry is authentic or not does not depend on the building in which a church happens to meet, nor on the quality of the music, nor on the entertainment factor. It does not depend on the spiritual 'high' generated, the numbers in attendance, the brand of coffee used, the quality of the biscuits, or the brilliance of the speaker. The marks of the Spirit's work are purity, knowledge, patience and kindness. The shape and form of Paul's ministry matched up to the message that he preached. There was a consistency in his credentials. He lived selflessly for the sake of Christ, he had purity of deeds and words, he was faithful through thick and thin, and he had a clear perspective. It is these that are the marks of authentic Christian ministry.

## 2. Change your allegiance (chapter 6 v. 11 to chapter 7 v. 4)

Having asked us to check our assessment, Paul then commands his readers to change their allegiance. Here he is asking the Corinthians to open themselves to him. And by opening themselves to him, to open themselves to the Christian Gospel and to Christian service. It is a profoundly emotive appeal, and Paul realises that because he is an ambassador of Jesus, if they were to distance themselves from him, then they would be also distancing themselves from salvation and the Lord Jesus Himself.

Paul makes his point in these verses with graphic appeals, using strong picture language. The first appeal is positive, the second negative.

### Embrace Authentic Ministry

The word translated in verses 11 and 13 as *widen* (in the context of hearts being opened wide) is a word used for building an extension. It may be an extension of a road (the Romans were forever widening their roads and developing their transport system), or the extension of a building. It is a picture everyone can associate with. Many have been involved in some form of home extension, and everyone has sat in traffic jams caused by road-widening projects.

Paul's concern is that the Corinthians make room in their hearts for him. Not just because he wants a few more addresses to add to his database, or because he wants to increase his own personal sphere of influence. His concern, as God's envoy, is that the Corinthians should recognise the authentic nature of his ministry, accept him, and in accepting him, so accept God Himself.

But it should be noticed that there is a negative to go with the positive. It is not simply a matter of positively opening our hearts to Paul with his message and ministry. If room is to be made in our hearts for Paul and his Gospel, there is no room for multiple occupancy. There have to be evictions, if there are to be admissions. It is therefore also a matter of turning away from other allegiances.

## Separate From Ungodliness

In verse 14, Paul makes the point very clearly, that Christians are to separate from unbelievers. He does this by use of a strong metaphor, alluding to the yoke used on a draught horse or ox. The picture is one of being wrongly joined in labour together with someone, or something. The statement has an identifiable Old Testament background. Firstly, the Greek word translated *unevenly yoked* in verse 14 is from the same word group as the word translated *different* in the Greek translation of Leviticus 19:19: *You shall not let your cattle breed with a different kind. You shall not sow your field with two kinds of seed, nor shall you wear a garment of cloth made of two different kinds of material.* Secondly, Deuteronomy 22:10 provides a specific prohibition on unequal yoking: *You shall not plough with an ox and a donkey together.*

The questions and quotations of verses 14 to 18 reinforce the impossibility of such a union. Five rhetorical questions highlight particular aspects of the fundamental differences between believers and unbelievers. *Righteousness* is contrasted to *lawlessness. Light* to *darkness. Christ* to *Belial* (evil people or the devil). Being part of the community of Christ to being separated from Him. The *temple of God* to *idols.*

Paul then shows such a separation to be rooted in God's promises and exhortations to His people in the Old Testament. In Leviticus 26:11-12 God promises to dwell with His people and to be their God, so anticipating believers being the temple of the living God: *I will make my dwelling among you, and my soul shall not abhor you. And I will walk among you and will be your God, and you shall be my people.* In Isaiah 52, it is in light of the LORD's salvation that His people are to *Depart, depart; go out from there; touch no unclean thing; go out from the midst of her; purify yourselves, you who bear the vessels of the LORD* (v. 11).

For the Corinthians, who have been flirting with immorality, and have had to have the 'severe letter' written to them commanding real repentance in the area of sexual immorality and their engagement with the world, Paul is saying 'do you not realise who you are through the Gospel?' If they are to realign with him and the Gospel of Jesus Christ, and so be reconciled to God, then there have to be evictions, as Christ comes in. This is a perfectly pitched appeal for a radical change of allegiance.

There needs to be clarity about what Paul is saying, and what he is not saying in these verses. Some have said that this is about relationships between Christians and non-Christians. To be clear, it is wrong for a Christian to marry a non-Christian person, but this verse is not first and foremost about that. Others have said that this is about entering into business partnerships with non-Christian people, but this passage is again not primarily about that. Rather, it is an appeal to our loves and our lifestyle, that we would not embrace the world, but rather cleanse ourselves from ungodly behaviour and living. To those caught up in worldly practices and lifestyle, which they know to run counter to the Gospel of the Lord Jesus Christ, Paul says *Make room in your hearts for us*, and *Be reconciled to God*. By observation from a number of years of Christian service, when people turn from authentic Christianity having been a member of a true church, they do not turn away to rank paganism. They turn away to a form of Christianity that knows none of the challenge of the Gospel of the Apostle Paul.

But by extension, inevitably, in the context of the whole letter, this also means distancing ourselves from ungodly teachers, and those who are encouraging ungodliness, even as they teach a different gospel to the Gospel that Paul teaches. The questions and quotations in verses 14 to 18 reinforce the impossibility of compromise on the issue. There can be no partnership, or fellowship, or agreement between the two. Christians are the temple of the living God, and so must be separate from the false teachers within the church as well as pagan worship outside of the church. There will always be men and women dressed up as Christian leaders on the fringes of Christian ministries who peddle a different gospel, encouraging people to embrace a lifestyle that the Lord Jesus rejects.

As Paul encourages this Corinthian church to distance itself from false teaching and false teachers, he is writing to the whole church family of Corinth, and not simply to the leadership. This requires serious thought for those of us in the denomination of the Church of England. The Church of England is of course a denomination, an organization of churches, and not strictly speaking a church itself. It has a foundational theology that is Reformed, Protestant and Biblical. It is common knowledge, however, that there are some within it who despise the teaching and the ministry of the Apostle Paul, and who want to change the teaching of the denomination. They have asked those who hold to the teaching and ministry of the Apostle Paul to engage in 'shared conversations' and come to 'good disagreements'. Personally, I consider it a profound folly to take seriously any shared conversation where the outcome is of 'good disagreement', with those who deny the ethical teaching of the Apostle Paul.

If they have to happen, shared conversations can be engaged in, but they cannot be undertaken naively. There is to be absolutely no suggestion at any point of spiritual allegiance in such an engagement with the denomination of the Church of England, or yoking together with those who have departed from the Apostle Paul. Engagement can be made as part of a legislative body, but there can be no suggestion of being joined together in spiritual work. According to Paul, we do not have the liberty to recognise as authentic disciples those who openly defy his teaching in an unrepentant way.

Holding fast to this principle will unavoidably impact relationships at both national and local levels. However, if no stand is taken, the younger generation will think the current leadership to be a fraud for their unwillingness to stand up and be counted. They will also be exceedingly unlikely to later take the necessary stands themselves. To the person who thinks that such exhortations are the preserve of grumpy old men, it must be remembered what is at stake. In so far as someone distances themselves from the Apostle Paul, they are also distancing themselves from Jesus Christ, and salvation.

## Conclusion

Having considered the Corinthians' relationship to Paul, at the close of this section we must ask ourselves what *we* make of Paul, and what place his message and his ministry have in *our* hearts. *Endurance* is the word that begins the list of commendations. The question is not, 'what did we once make of Paul?' Rather, it is, 'what do we make of him *now*?' If we think he's just a bit extreme with all this suffering and hard work, we need to reassess our understanding of authentic ministry. If we would rather have a more dramatic and flashy style of church, that seems on the surface to be more spiritual, we probably have not understood the message. If we are looking to accommodate our message to the world, and just soften the edges, so that we proclaim a different message, whether at the school gate, or in the office, we need to correct our view of ministry.

We must be rigorous in evicting any wrong ideas about ministry that may have just crept in, and instead embrace wholeheartedly the work of Paul the Apostle. His concern here is for the local church, and today we must work to ensure that, rather than slipping or drifting into an alternative form and shape of Christian ministry, we are fully aligned with him.

## Questions

1. How does our culture assess the ministry credentials that Paul presents?
2. Why might we find it difficult to align ourselves with a ministry exhibiting these credentials today?
3. Where might you need to separate from false teachers and false teaching today?
4. How do the promises of chapter 6 verses 16 to 18 encourage you to stay aligned with the Apostle Paul?

# Bibliography

Barnett, Paul. *The Second Epistle to the Corinthians.* The New International Commentary on the New Testament. Grand Rapids, Mich: W.B. Eerdmans Pub, 1997.

Bowler, Kate. *Blessed: A History of the American Prosperity Gospel.* New York: Oxford University Press, 2013.

Carroll, Lewis. *Alice's adventures in wonderland ; & Through the looking glass, and what Alice found there.* London: Collector's Library, 2004.

Guthrie, George H. *2 Corinthians.* Baker Exegetical Commentary on the New Testament. Grand Rapids, Michigan: Baker Academic a division of Baker Publishing Group, 2015.

Lewis, C. S. *The Screwtape letters.* London: Fount, 1998.

Torrey, R.A. *How to work for Christ: a compendium of effective methods.* London: James Nisbet & Co, 1901.

# About the Authors

William Taylor served in the British Army from 1983-88. Having studied at Ridley Hall, Cambridge he was ordained in 1991 and subsequently appointed curate at Christ Church, Bromley. In 1995 he joined St Helen's, Bishopsgate, an historic church in the City of London, where he became the Rector in 1998. He is married to Janet, and they have three children – Emily, Digby and Archie.

David Dargue qualified as an accountant with Ernst & Young LLP in 2005, before doing the Associate Scheme and then serving in the City ministry at St Helen's, Bishopsgate. After further training at Oak Hill College, he joined Christ Church Newcastle in 2014, most recently serving as Minister of Christ Church Gosforth. He is married to Sarah, and they have three children – Toby, Emily & Sam.